SALT WATER FISHING

MARK SOSIN
AND
GEORGE POVEROMO

OUTDOOR ASSOCIATES
BOOKS

Published by

OUTDOOR ASSOCIATES, INC.
14155 North Miami Avenue
North Miami, Florida 33168

PRINTED IN THE UNITED STATES OF AMERICA

ISBN 0-945443-00-5

CONTENTS

ABOUT THE AUTHORS

Recognized as an authority on marine angling with emphasis on both tactics and tackle, MARK SOSIN has fished extensively for most major game fish in more than 40 countries on five continents. His well-researched presentations have appeared in leading magazines, daily newspapers, on radio, and in an impressive number of important books and fishing films. He currently hosts the award-winning, nationally-televised "Mark Sosin's Salt Water Journal."

Sosin is a Past President of the Outdoor Writers Association of America, holds membership in the American Society of Journalists and Authors, as well as the Society of Professional Journalists, and has been elected to the International Fishing Hall of Fame.

GEORGE POVEROMO is no stranger to salt water fishing actively pursuing his sport since he was old enough to grasp a rod and reel. He has fished extensively in the Atlantic Ocean and Gulf of Mexico, Southern California and the Baja, Hawaii the Bahamas, and a number of Central and South American countries. As Salt Water Sportsman Magazine's Field Editor, he continues to challenge a variety of gamefish in national and international waters. Aside from an in-depth knowledge of the sport and its techniques, he maintains an equally comprehensive background in boating and conservation. His work has appeared in a number of national publications including Outdoor Life, Field & Stream, and Fishing World. Aside from his writings, George is a consultant to several major marine manufacturers.

THE CONCEPT OF FISHING

Fishing is just as much a mental exercise as it is a physical activity. Those who excel and produce consistent results in terms of fish caught don't harbor deep, dark secrets nor have they discovered a panacea known only to them and their quarry. Instead, the men and women who always seem to catch more than their share are serious students of the sport. They become impressively observant on the water and willingly modify techniques to meet any situation encountered.

Equally important, every competent angler is well-schooled in the fundamentals of this discipline. There is no such thing as thinking like a fish; fish react to most situations instinctively rather than going through a process of reasoning. The key lies in understanding the habits of your quarry and the habitat in which it lives.

Fish try to remain relatively comfortable in terms of temperature, salinity, water clarity, depth, and so forth. Each species tries to establish its own niche in the environment as a means of reducing competition for food and habitat. Primarily, an individual must take in enough food to survive, avoid becoming a meal for something else, and reproduce to insure continuation of the species. That's all that nature demands.

Behavior patterns of fish lack the complexity that many anglers want to assign to the problem. Unfortunately, most of us simply do not understand what fish do or what triggers a response in them and automatically assume it is complicated. A skilled skipper in the northeast knows that if he positions his boat properly and tosses fresh chum in the water, he will attract gamefish behind his boat. Day after day, the procedure seldom varies. His counterpart on the tropical flats understands the importance of tidal stage to fish movements and regularly predicts when fish will appear. There is nothing mysterious or mystical about this. He has observed the same occurrence time after time and knows it usually happens. To the person who doesn't understand the techniques of chumming or has no knowledge of tides, the complexity of the event staggers the mind.

Fishing is a game of inches. If one were to analyze the methods used by those who score consistently and compare them to the actions of fishermen with poorer results, the differences would be minor. All of us have seen times when two anglers standing side by side and using identical lures have totally opposite experiences. One may catch most of the fish, while his partner struggles to hook anything. Obviously, the first angler is doing something the second one isn't or he is not doing something that his friend is. That subtle difference spells victory or defeat.

Most species in the marine environment are opportunity feeders. They know instinctively that a food source is not going to remain in the area until they get hungry or decide to eat. If a fish looks at an offering and does not respond immediately, you should begin to suspect that something may be wrong with it and monitor the bait or lure even more closely. A couple of refusals should convince you to try something else.

Experienced anglers operate on the theory that fish are looking at their bait constantly and that there are more fish in a given area than one might think. If nothing happens within a reasonable period, they will change offerings and eventually seek out another spot.

Leading fishermen have uncanny memories. They remember all types of situations and an incredible number of specific catches. Not only are they able to recall these events and benefit from them, but they constantly monitor everything they are doing at the moment. If a strike occurs on a lure, they know how deep the artificial was and the retrieve they were using. Nothing is done at random; actions are planned and then executed. Many anglers maintain extensive logs with entries reflecting every day they spent on the water. Referring to these pages often helps to salvage a day when conditions are less than ideal and one has to work hard for a few fish.

No book can school the reader in dedication to details or hone one's powers of observation on the water. Awareness comes with practice and experience. The written word provides the starting point by stressing fundamentals as well as advanced concepts. Understanding the mechanics of the sport becomes the prerequisite for success in the field.

Perhaps the most important concept centers on convincing the beginner that if he is off the mark, it probably isn't by very much. Remember that most marine species are opportunistic feeders and will pursue a variety of natural baits as well as artificials.

The primary step lies in locating the fish. Once you have found your quarry, catching it may not be as difficult as you suspect. There is no substitute for actual experience. The more you fish, the better you become.

A growing legion of anglers continue to turn to ocean and estuary, believing that the vastness of the seas contains an endless well of fish populations. In recent years, we are learning that the stocks of many gamefish, once taken for granted, have been depleted and are seriously threatened. With more fishermen depending on these finite resources and using increasingly sophisticated techniques, there will be fewer fish to catch unless the world becomes successful in management methods coupled with a serious concern. For that reason, we have chosen to place the conservation chapter first in this book instead of last. We urge you to read it and put conservation first in your attitude and actions both on and off the water. Unless all of us work together toward protecting our marine resources on a continuous basis, glowing stories of the "good old days" will be based on truth instead of dimness of memory.

Water Temperature Ranges for Salt Water Fish

The table lists water temperatures applicable to many of the more popular salt water game fish species. Under the *Lower* heading are temperatures which a particular species tends to avoid, although it might swim through water colder than that indicated. Similarly, under *Upper* are temperatures which the fish normally shun. The *Range* column lists temperature limits which are most favorable for angling.

Both Fahrenheit (F) & Celsius (C) readings are given since water temperatures obtained from governmental s[atellites] normally are given in the latter only.

Note that ocean surface water temperatures may va[ry] considerably from those at greater depths and such varia[tions] should be taken into account when actually fishi[ng]. Thus a tilefish, feeding in 500 feet of water ranging arou[nd] 55°F, may be found when the surface is well above t[hat] temperature.

SPECIES	LOWER	UPPER	RANGE
Albacore (Thunnus alalunga)	59°F / 15°C	67°F / 19°C	62°-65°F / 16°-18°C
Amberjack (Seriola dumerili)	60°F / 16°C	72°F / 22°C	63°-67°F / 17°-19°C
Barracuda, Atlantic (Sphyraena barracuda)	65°F / 18°C	90°F / 32°C	75°-85°F / 24°-29°C
Barracuda, Pacific (Sphyraena argentia)	54°F / 12°C	71°F / 22°C	64°-67°F / 18°-19°C
Bass, Black Sea (Centropristes striatus)	48°F / 9°C	85°F / 29°C	60°-70°F / 16°-21°C
Bass, Kelp (Paralabrax clathratus)	62°F / 16°C	73°F / 23°C	65°-68°F / 18°-20°C
Bass, Striped (Morone saxatilis)	40°F / 5°C	80°F / 27°C	45°-65°F / 7°-18°C
Bass, White Sea (Cynoscion nobilis)	58°F / 14°C	75°F / 23°C	65°-69°F / 18°-21°C
Bluefish (Pomatomus saltatrix)	50°F / 10°C	84°F / 29°C	62°-70°F / 18°-21°C
Bonefish (Albula vulpes)	68°F / 20°C	90°F / 32°C	72°-82°F / 22°-27°C
Bonito, Atlantic (Sarda sarda)	57°F / 14°C	72°F / 22°C	63°-67°F / 16°-19°C
Bonito, Pacific (Sarda chiliensis)	59°F / 15°C	74°F / 23°C	64°-68°F / 18°-20°C
Cobia (Rachycentron canadus)	55°F / 12°C	82°F / 27°C	66°-72°F / 19°-22°C
Cod (Gadus morhua)	32°F / 0°C	59°F / 15°C	44°-49°F / 6°-8°C
Croaker (Micropogon undulatus)	41°F / 5°C	85°F / 29°C	60°-70°F / 16°-21°C
Dolphin (Coryphaena hippurus)	69°F / 21°C	80°F / 27°C	73°-77°F / 23°-25°C
Drum, Black (Pogonias cromis)	55°F / 12°C	90°F / 32°C	68°-74°F / 20°-23°C
Drum, Red (Channel Bass) (Sciaenops ocellata)	59°F / 15°C	85°F / 29°C	69°-73°F / 21°-23°C
Flounder, Summer (Fluke) (Paralichthys dentatus)	69°F / 21°C	80°F / 27°C	73°-77°F / 23°-25°C
Flounder, Winter (Pseudopleuronectes americanus)	35°F / 2°C	60°F / 16°C	48°-52°F / 9°-11°C
Haddock (Melanogramus aeglefinus)	36°F / 2°C	52°F / 11°C	45°-50°F / 7°-9°C
Jack Crevalle (Caranx hippos)	65°F / 18°C	85°F / 29°C	70°-78°F / 21°-25°C
Mackerel, Atlantic (Scomber scrombrus)	45°F / 7°C	70°F / 21°C	60°-65°F / 18°-20°C
Mackerel, King (Scomberomorus cavalla)	70°F / 21°C	88°F / 31°C	74°-79°F / 23°-26°C
Mackerel, Pacific (Pneumatophorus diego)	47°F / 9°C	70°F / 21°C	56°-62°F / 13°-16°C
Mackerel, Spanish (Scomberomorus maculatus)	68°F / 20°C	85°F / 29°C	72°-80°F / 22°-27°C
Marlin, Black (Makaira indicus)	70°F / 21°C	87°F / 30°C	75°-79°F / 24°-26°C

SPECIES	LOWER	UPPER	RAN[GE]
Marlin, Blue (Makaira nigricans)	69°F / 21°C	88°F / 31°C	75°-8... / 24°-2...
Marlin, Striped (Tetrapturus audax)	61°F / 16°C	78°F / 25°C	68°-7... / 20°-2...
Marlin, White (Tetrapturus albidus)	62°F / 16°C	84°F / 29°C	66°-7... / 19°-2...
Permit (Trachinotus falcatus)	67°F / 19°C	85°F / 29°C	70°-7... / 21°-2...
Pollock (Pollachius virens)	33°F / 1°C	60°F / 15°C	44°-5... / 6°-1...
Pompano (Trachinotus cardinus)	68°F / 20°C	85°F / 29°C	75°-8... / 21°-2...
Sailfish (Istiophorus platyperus)	70°F / 21°C	88°F / 31°C	76°-8... / 24°-2...
Scup (Porgy) (Stenotomus versicolor)	42°F / 6°C	73°F / 23°C	57°-6... / 14°-1...
Seatrout (Spotted Weakfish) (Cynoscion nebulosus)	62°F / 16°C	90°F / 32°C	70°-7... / 21°-2...
Shark, Blue (Prionace glauca)	55°F / 12°C	73°F / 23°C	60°-6... / 15°-2...
Shark, Mako (Isurus oxyrinchus)	60°F / 15°C	78°F / 25°C	65°-7... / 18°-2...
Sheepshead (Archosargus probatocephalus)	60°F / 15°C	78°F / 25°C	65°-7... / 18°-2...
Snapper, Red (Lutjanus campechanus)	50°F / 10°C	64°F / 18°C	55°-6... / 13°-1...
Snook (Centropomus undecimalis)	62°F / 16°C	90°F / 32°C	75°-8... / 23°-3...
Spot (Leiostomus xanthurus)	60°F / 15°C	95°F / 35°C	70°-8... / 21°-2...
Swordfish (Xiphias gladius)	50°F / 10°C	78°F / 25°C	64°-6... / 18°-2...
Tarpon (Megalops atlantica)	72°F / 22°C	90°F / 32°C	75°-8... / 24°-3...
Tautog (Blackfish) (Tautoga onitis)	60°F / 16°C	76°F / 24°C	68°-7... / 20°-2...
Tilefish (Lopholatilus chamaeleonticeps)	48°F / 9°C	59°F / 15°C	50°-5... / 10°-1...
Tuna, Bigeye (Thunnus obesus)	55°F / 13°C	68°F / 20°C	60°-6... / 15°-1...
Tuna, Blackfin (Thunnus atlanticus)	70°F / 21°C	82°F / 27°C	72°-7... / 22°-2...
Tuna, Bluefin (Thunnus thynnus)	50°F / 10°C	82°F / 27°C	61°-6... / 16°-1...
Tuna, Skipjack (Euthynnus pelamis)	55°F / 13°C	75°F / 23°C	60°-7... / 15°-2...
Tuna, Yellowfin (Thunnus albacares)	60°F / 15°C	80°F / 27°C	73°-7... / 23°-2...
Wahoo (Ancanthocybium solandri)	68°F / 20°C	85°F / 29°C	72°-8... / 22°-2...
Weakfish (Cynoscion regalis)	55°F / 13°C	78°F / 25°C	68°-7... / 20°-2...
Yellowtail, Pacific (Seriola dorsalis)	60°F / 15°C	72°F / 22°C	64°-6... / 18°-2...

Courtesy: Hal Lyman, Salt Water Spor[tsman]

THE SERIOUS SIDE

...olphin provide exciting sport for blue water anglers. During ...e heat of battle, it's easy to forget and take too many. If you ...n't release unneeded fish, move off and leave the school.

...ecreational fishing has grown to unparalleled heights within ...e past decade. There are more boats, tackle, and fishing-...lated accessories marketed and sold than ever before, and ...ere are no apparent signs of this progression slowing. While ...arter boat captains, tackle and boat manufacturers, their ...stributors and dealers, and consumers continue to enjoy the ...enefits of this expanding sport, there needs to be a better ...nderstanding of the environment we are tapping. With a ...owing number of pressures being placed on the fishery, it's ...ore important than ever before to wisely utilize our ...sources.

THE PROBLEMS

There are numerous problems facing our fishery. While it ...ems the finger can be pointed at a specific cause, partic-...arly when it's directly associated with our favorite gamefish, ...s often the combination of a series of perplexities that lead to ...e decline of a fishery. Habitat destruction is a major issue, ...hich has a dramatic effect on inshore, coastal, and even reef ...h. Consider the Florida snook. Here is a species that thrived ...the southern portion of the state during the late 1950s and ...rly 60's. From the late 1960's a serious decline was noted, ...aching startling population reductions between the mid ...70s and early 1980s. Among the many problems facing this ...opular gamefish is the loss of habitat.

Snook spawn in and around inlets during a spring tide. ...eir eggs and larvae then float back into the estuaries with ...ter containing a salinity of 27 to 35 parts per thousand and, ...a critical point, will sink as the salinity decreases below 27 ...rts per thousand. The eggs will then hatch and the fry

become dependent upon the environment over the first two years of their life. The filling in of wetlands and the loss of vital nursing grounds to construction are having a severe impact on snook populations. Also, controlled dumping of fresh water, practiced primarily on Florida's east coast, alters the optimum salinity levels needed for proper reproduction.

As condominiums, houses, and thriving populations, continue to rapidly replace mangrove marshes, insecticides are employed to control mosquitos. Aerial spraying of organic phosphate chemicals such as Baytex and Malathion on Florida's west coast, is having a profound effect on the species. Because the snook egg is a floater and within 48 hours of its fertilization will soften and become very susceptible to taking in chemicals, its contact with the poison, which has a tendency to remain on the water's surface, results in death and malformations.

The snook is not the only major gamefish suffering from a lack of estuary management. The striped bass is another fish whose over exploitation has taxed a stressed environment to support (unsuccessfully) adequate juvenile populations. Stripers spawn in tidal rivers and estuaries with waters containing a salinity of less than one part per thousand. The eggs are carried back and forth with tidal fluctuations for approximately 72 hours. After hatching, the fry will carry and consume a yoke sac for about four days before feeding in the wild. It's at this stage where biologists are discovering a major die off. Acid rain, agricultural run-off, pesticides, and industrial pollution are some of the suspects. If the fish pass this critical stage, they'll be approximately 6 millimeters in size and establish the year class. A more normal mortality rate is experienced after this point.

The Potomac River may lend substance to the above suspicions. This river received detrimental amounts of pollution as it flowed through metropolitan areas, enough to severely limit local striped bass spawning. Through stricter dumping regulations and a major clean-up project aimed at the river, the Potomac is now experiencing a revitalization of the fishery. The improved water quality is responsible for an increase in local striped bass populations and aquatic weeds.

Habitat destruction affects virtually all forms of marine life. The increasing loss of mangroves to development in Florida is having a startling effect on not only gamefish, but other vital species as well. The once abundant mullet, whose fall migration down the beaches of the east coast often spanned many miles and turned the water's surface black, have now been reduced to occasional flurries at unpredictable intervals. While the mullet's value may not be readily apparent, it weighs heavily when you consider that they constitute a primary link in the food chain of fish such as tarpon, snook, jacks, sharks, mackerel, kingfish and even sailfish and dolphin. As their numbers shrink, so does the forage for other fish. The end result is a reduction of fish, whose numbers are based on the environment's ability to support them.

POLLUTION

Another important function of estuaries, and one often overlooked by its destroyers, is their ability to filter out impurities. Similar to an automobile's oil filter, estuaries rid foreign substances from waters washing through the systems. By removing this natural vegetation, you'll not only subject that portion of the environment to pollution, but also stress any grass flats or oyster bars that receive its water.

Pollution is by no means limited to insecticides and estuary damage. It's a problem that exists in various forms on all coasts. Offshore dumping sites, where unmeasurable amounts of both industrial and human waste are pumped daily into the ocean for absorption, are still basically going unregulated. Theoretically positioned far enough at sea to prevent the discharge from drifting inshore and posing a threat to humans, these outlets have gravely imperiled their surrounding environments. One such example is a dumping ground some 14 1/2 miles off Long Branch, New Jersey known as the Acid Waste Disposal Site. Decades of releasing sulfuric and hydrochloric acids have nullified the immediate area of sea life, leaving its calling card of a brown stain or discoloration on the water's surface. It's not exactly the healthiest environment for brine shrimp, marine plankton, and other vital links of the food chain.

Tons of primary and secondary sewage pour out of ocean disposal sites daily. Experts who have monitored their impact report that they have destroyed the natural bottom by blanketing it with settling sludge. Placed in areas that once supported healthy ecosystems that annually attracted migrations of fish, these dump sites have experienced a dramatic reduction in life. What's worse is that strong currents, severe storms, and eddies can absorb the poisons, spreading them to other regions. And if man-made disposal sites weren't placing enough stress offshore, freighters hauling fuel and oil have been known to clean their reservoirs at sea. While its against Federal Law to do so, the lack of man power to enforce the regulation gives the freighters an upper hand. Just as the snook eggs and striped bass fry are highly susceptible to contaminants, so are the eggs and juveniles of most offshore species.

A natural pollution which affects humans more than fish is also becoming more visible in the southeastern United States due to the mistreatment of the environment. Ciguatera is a nerve poison caused by a microscopic plant (dinoflagellate organism) that attaches itself to algae on coral reefs. The organisms multiply when the reef is damaged, which usually results from ships anchoring and breaking off portions of it. The smaller fish consume the organisms, passing them along to any larger fish to which they may fall prey. The poison has little effect on sea life. Yet, a human will contract the painful illness when he consumes a fish containing the toxin, which may take upward of a year before it passes through his system. To date, there is no cure for ciguatera. Fortunately, there is a growing concern about protecting natural reefs from destruction. John Pennekamp Park in the upper Florida Keys has installed mooring buoys on their reefs, requiring dive and fishing boats to use them. Through this system, they have insured the reef against further destruction and ultimately, ciguatera.

COMMERCIAL OVERFISHING

The basically unregulated destruction of vital fish stocks progresses at a rapid rate. Governing bodies continue to rely on crisis management over common sense when it comes to addressing such issues. That is, they'll wait until a stock collapses before making any adjustments. Even then, there are examples where the mayhem is allowed to continue. Two painful examples of crisis management have surfaced in recent years. The king mackerel was once a prolific fish that invaded South Florida during the winter months, and its southwest coast during the spring and fall. Due to the arrival of roller rig boats that intercepted the stocks as they migrated into the regions, king mackerel have been virtually removed from the fishery in several short years.

The annual kingfish run supported a healthy charter, recreational, and hook and line commercial fishery on both coasts. Large smoker kings exceeding 20 pounds were available to anglers working live baits around nearshore depressions, channel edges, and over the reefs, while schooling fish in various sizes often became so numerous that they were cursed by anglers trying to live bait sailfish. In fact, the density of the schools provided perfect opportunities to use a variety of tackle, including fly. While the South Florida coast offers a broad range of fish to pursue, the southwest's economy relies heavily on the annual passage of kingfish and mackerel.

The fishery that resident and visiting anglers became so fond of came to an end shortly after the roller rigs took over. The decline of kingfish stocks on Florida's west coast eliminated a once thriving charter boat industry and put many hook and line commercial fishermen out of work. The east coast catch also declined dramatically, forcing anglers to concentrate their efforts on other species. In addition to the kingfish, mackerel also fell victims to the netters, who routinely employed spotter planes to direct them to schooling fish. Ironically, a good portion of the catches were shipped to foreign countries and not even utilized in the United States. An enterprising fleet of roller rig boats whose backers possess enough dollars and political clout to prevent sensible regulations, have dealt a near fatal blow to this crowd-pleasing fish.

Spurned by an overnight craze for cajun style blackened fish, redfish fillets quickly climbed up the rankings from an almost undesirable product to one challenging the prices of grouper and snapper. A major advertising firm couldn't have done a better marketing job in promoting the popularity of this coarse fish than the one by the commercial industry. The rules of the game are the same as for kingfish: spotter planes and roller rigs, although the location shifted slightly to the Gulf of Mexico where the large, ocean run or brood stock reds migrate.

Scientists tell us that a redfish doesn't reach sexual maturity until it is about five or six years old or approximately between 15 and 20 pounds. Most of the reds taken by recreational anglers in Gulf Coast estuaries such as the Chandeleur Islands off Louisiana and the Florida Everglades, haven't spawned. As the fish grow larger and become sexually active, they'll move out of the sounds, bays and estuaries, and join with stocks of breeders out in the Gulf. After a successful spawn, the larvae will develop and depend on the estuaries.

The damaging blows come from the hands of netters as they remove tons of prime brood stock redfish, which jeopardize the future of the species. The flesh of fish averaging between 20 and 50 pounds in weight is very coarse and low

Netting of brood stock and overfishing have threatened the populations of redfish in the Gulf of Mexico. This beauty taken on light spinning is about to be released.

quality compared to a much younger fish. Yet, oversized specimens are a netters dream; large schools in open water that are easy to round up. Within short order, a fleet of about six or seven boats have just about crippled a once healthy breeding supply of fish. In one instance, it was reported that a netter had just filled his boat's hold and radioed his whereabouts to another netter. As a friendly gesture, the captain decided he would set and pull his net on a school of reds, holding them until the other ship arrived to load the catch in vacant boxes. The friend never showed. An estimated 50,000 pounds of dead and dying redfish were left for the sharks.

Fortunately, due in part to the heroic efforts of the Coastal Conservation Association, some regulations were formed to prevent the harvest of breeding size reds. Several states on the Gulf Coast have passed "no sale" provisions, eliminating the boats from bartering their catch at the respective shores. There's an increasing national awareness of the redfish's plight and, as of this writing, gamefish status for the fish is pending in Florida. A gamefish declaration protects a species from harvest.

THE BILLFISH PROBLEM

Once abundant in Florida waters, the broadbill swordfish is a prime example of how efficient offshore longlining can be. In 1976, a nighttime swordfishery was discovered off Miami Beach, Florida. Due to the high mercury content of swordfish, the effort was limited mostly to an increasing number of recreational anglers. During that brief heyday, it wasn't unusual for an angler, drifting with illuminated squid, to catch at least one and as many as four broadbills a night. The fish weighed an average of 250 pounds and often soared over 500 pounds.

When the Federal Government raised the acceptable mercury levels, the U.S. longlining fleet was quick to respond. In four years, they had the South Florida swordfishery in grave danger. The number of fish captured per set went down dramatically as did their average weight. Today, the fishery is in poor shape not only off South Florida, but other regions as well. The longliners were so proficient in their job that many of them are now working major breeding grounds in the Caribbean. The current average weight of a swordfish stands at 40 pounds.

As its name implies, a longline is a stretch of heavy monofilament that can span from a 1/4 of a mile to over 15 miles. Dropper hooks, varying in lengths, are attached to the main line at regular intervals. Commercial boats usually bait and set the hooks in a shallow to deep pattern at sunset, retrieving the gear by sun up. The larger boats are capable of fishing three or four longlines per night.

The longline is non-selective in that it catches sharks, billfish, dolphin, wahoo, and tuna. While billfish and tuna are taken by longliners at night, they tend to feed heavily during the day, especially the early morning and late afternoon hours. The current craze for mesquite grilled yellowfin tuna has caused its market price to skyrocket, prompting American longliners to make day sets for them. Naturally, the daytime effort will have a considerable effect on both white and blue marlin; more so than the night shift. What's worse is that there's more emphasis on starting a market for billfish in the states not protecting them, primarily because the more popular food fish species have been decimated to the point where it's becoming less feasible to commercially fish for them.

The white marlin market in the northeastern U.S. is expanding annually, while blue marlin is becoming a somewhat common sight on the "fresh catch" chalkboards of several coastal restaurants. Maine recently passed a "no sale" provision on white marlin, setting a precedent for neighboring states. Florida protects the sailfish from commercial exploitation through a gamefish status, but not so with the marlins.

Too many sharks and barracuda are killed because they have teeth. These valuable predators should be released. Use a gaff through the lower jaw to hold the fish and cut the hook if necessary.

Until the Federal Government is willing to regulate the longline industry, expect to see an increase in fishing pressures from both the American and foreign vessels, particularly in the tuna and billfish rich Gulf of Mexico.

GILL NETS

Gill nets are harsh, non-selective commercial tools that leave widespread destruction and controversy in their wake. Southern California is only one state that has a major problem with this booming fishery. Over 1,000 permits are currently in use. A gill net is a webbing, usually monofilament or plastic, that's suspended vertically in the water by surface floats and weights on its bottom, entangling the gill plates or bodies of fish that swim into it. They can be anchored or adjusted to drift. Drift gill nets are targeted to intercept pelagic species and constitute a fairly inexpensive way of catching them.

Two major concerns arise from the use of a gill net. Whereas the longline relies on a fish to eat a bait, the gill net takes anything that can't slip through its mesh. And chances are that any fish escaping will do so with a considerable amount of effort and suffer mortal wounds from abrasion or dismemberment. This non-selective gear continually takes the lives of sharks, whales, porpoise, sea lions, countless numbers of billfish, and even birds. The other problem comes from lost gear, which continually floats along claiming sealife. The heavy webbing, particularly plastic, can stay intact for years.

FISH TRAPS

Similar to a drift net, a fish trap is an indiscriminate killer that also poses a threat if lost. Fish traps are wire mesh cages with a flexible, funnel-tapered entry, designed primarily for grouper and snapper. These weighted traps are baited and positioned over rocky structure or reefs where the targeted fish are likely to be. Fish enter the cage by sliding through the chamber and are captured. The chances of working their way back out of the narrow end of the beam are slim.
The majority of the catch is rarely grouper and snapper,

but rather an assortment of tropical fish having little or no food value. They are often dead or dying by the time they're retrieved, a result of making repeated contacts with the wire mesh cage in an effort to escape. A lost trap continues to kill, since any dead or decaying fish always attracts new victims, continuing its vicious cycle. In addition to fish traps, bottom longlines are used to harvest grouper. Considering the slow growth attained by a grouper, it's almost amazing that they still exist in fishable quantities.

NEW PROBLEM

The latest species under commercial fire is the Greater amberjack. Similar to the redfish, the amberjack is known more for its dogged fighting characteristics than its tablefare. In fact, tail segments of the fish are often infested with parasites. The decline of customary food species creates markets for new flesh. This problem is not only surfacing in the Gulf of Mexico, but in South Florida and the Keys, where the fish are literally being winched aboard commercial boats via electric reels. Amberjack concentrate and spawn over structure during the spring and early summer, making them very susceptible to overfishing. While they can still be counted on to save an otherwise unproductive fishing day, there may come a time in the near future when they'll be just an incidental catch unless something is done to curb this problem.

GREAT SOLUTION

Ironically, the National Marine Fisheries Service is pushing hard to popularize underutilized species, encouraging fishermen to target monkfish, grunts, sheepshead, etc. It's not that these fish don't provide fun, sport, and good tablefare. They do. It just seems funny how the popular species have about vanished through mismanagement, forcing a sharper focus on these other fish. What do we fish for when the secondary species are wiped out?

RECREATIONAL EXPLOITATION

As hard and heavy as the commercial pressures continue

Shark fishing gives anglers a chance to battle heavyweights anywhere along the coast. These animals take a long time t reproduce and grow, so they should be released. Cutting the wire leader is all it requires to set a shark free.

to be on our fishery, the recreational angler does more than his fair share of damage. While this trend has been changing somewhat in recent years, there are still many fishermen who judge a successful day by the contents of their fish box. In addition, more recreational anglers are selling their catch, adding to the overall pressures on fish stocks. A charter boat captain who sells only enough fish to keep his operating expenses down is in an understandable position, providing he keeps within a respectable limit. It's when the recreational fisherman, who holds down a full time job outside of the marine industry, decides to sell his catch that questions arise.

It doesn't take long at a dock, marina or boat ramp to single out this class of fisherman. He's the one with several large coolers, running long and hard to productive areas to fill them up. He not only does an injustice to his sport, but competes with commercial hook and liners who are in the business to make a living. Somehow, the "sport" and enjoyment of fishing seem to get lost in the race for the almighty dollar. The irony of the situation is that the money he makes selling fish is not critical to his well being or life style.

When you analyze the number of recreational anglers on the water during a prime weekend, the amount of baits in the water, and fish boated, the figures can be astounding. Perhaps the best way to resolve this upswing in fish peddling is for the coastal states to enact laws that prohibit an angler from selling seafood unless he derives a major portion of his income from commercial fishing.

TOURNAMENTS

Although they may appear to be fun, fishing tournaments are placing incredible amounts of pressure on local fisheries. When a competition awards significant purses for catching the largest quantity of fish, it is forcing competitors to fish longer and harder than they may normally do otherwise. Add to that the high dollar side bets or calcuttas of most major billfish tournaments and you're practically guaranteed of a fish kill to verify winning claims.

Some "sportfishing" tournaments go so far as to require their anglers to turn over all eligible fish to the committees, regardless of size. They'll be trucked off to the local fish processing house and sold to further a promoter's income. Think about it. What better way to branch into the commercial fishery than to have other people use their own boats, burn their own fuel, expend their energy, and then turn their catch over to you at the day's end. There's very little overhead, except the effort it takes to secure a few major sponsors to front the prize and operations monies.

Then, there are those contests that target stressed species, such as Florida kingfish tournaments, and waste those that have little or no food value. With the snook population of South Florida in dire straits, one obviously well-informed promoter tried to feature them in a kill tournament. There are still tournaments that practice the needless killing of tarpon, billfish, barracuda and sharks, with prizes ranging from a plaque to considerable amounts of cash. •

Not all fishing tournaments are bad. With the growing concern for conservation, many billfish competitions are going to a release format, particularly in the south. Logistics have been worked out where major amounts of cash and billfish release events can go hand in hand. Either through the use of observers on large boats or polygraph exams for the small boat competitions, scoring claims can be checked just as accurately, if not more so, than by requiring fish to be dragged back to the dock. Many non-billfish tournaments are now applying sensible minimum weights and daily bag limits to reduce fishing mortality. By emphasizing quality over quantity, these promoters aim to keep fishing mortality at a reasonable level.

Trying to convince an angler not to enter a tournament will not work, especially if he has a chance to make a few dollars at the expense of dead fish. Even if he is conservation minded, an attractive amount of cash will often override his better judgement. The solution lies in the hands of the event's sponsors. By utilizing their money to fund only those competitions that are conservation governed, and where a percentage of the income goes back into an environment enhancement project, the manufacturers can dictate the necessary changes to the promoter. If a promoter refuses to alter his rules, the sponsor simply looks for another event to support. There are certainly plenty of tournaments that would love to secure a major sponsorship.

THE SOLUTIONS

The problems listed above are only a broad sampling of those facing our environment. However, there's no need for despair. With proper planning and a good attitude, there are

A release gaff slipped through the lower jaw of a fish enables one to handle his quarry prior to turning it loose. If possible, keep the fish from thrashing against the boat until it settles down.

Center console boats have opened the world of offshore angling to more and more people. This team is ready to release a blu[e] marlin after taking the appropriate photos of their prize.

ways to insure the future of our fisheries. By adhering to a few rules of general sportsmanship, you can do your part for the resource.

Anglers are now becoming aware of the need to release fish, hopefully allowing them to spawn again before they are recaptured. There's a need to place more emphasis on quality catches (rather than quantity), and the number of fish released, rather than layering a cooler with them. Anglers also must learn to keep only enough fish for a few fresh dinners and release any surplus, even if they are prime food species. A frozen fish isn't as tasty as a fresh fillet, and it often ends up lost in the back of a freezer only to be discarded several months later.

By selecting your tackle with thought, you can also aim to reduce fish mortality. Many anglers are now using bronze-plated hooks over stainless steel, because they tend to rust away quickly in a salt water environment. If a fish breaks free or has swallowed a live bait, the hook should disintegrate within several days, giving the fish a greater chance of survival. There's been plenty of controversy lately over the use of live bait in billfishing, with the major argument being that the livies are easily swallowed in comparison to a rigged bait or lure. While this fact is true, mortality levels are often increased by improperly handling a fish at boatside.

If a fish has swallowed a live bait and the intent is to release it, carefully grab the bill near its base with your thumbs facing each other. This grip will lend greater control of the fish and you will maintain the ability to push it away from the boat if it decides to leap. Once the fish is subdued, remove the hook, or clip the leader close to the fish's mouth, if he has swallowed it. Never try to snap the leader by quickly jerking on it because it'll only rip the fish's innards, prompting internal bleeding and death. Reviving a worn out fish can be as simple as placing the boat in gear and forcing water through its gills.

CONSERVATION

Benthic fish such as sea bass, groupers, snappers, an[d] amberjack that are quickly pumped up from the depths usuall[y] have inflated air bladders resulting from the drastic changes i[n] ascending pressures. Unaided, they are nearly impossible t[o] return to their lairs. Slightly puncturing the bladder with an ic[e] pick or another small, sharp object will relieve the pressur[e] and enable a fish to return to bottom. Air bladders penetrat[e] through the mouths of groupers and snappers. Amberjack[s] require a slight puncture behind a pectoral fin and just belo[w] the lateral line.

Off the water, make sure to support groups that ar[e] concerned with proper fisheries management. Do som[e] research and check up on the organizations packing th[e] heavier punches. The Coastal Conservation Association an[d] its affiliates have been doing a commendable job. And if th[e] revenues of a salt water fishing license will be used to enhanc[e] or protect the resources, go for it. Also, support senator[s,] governors, and even presidential candidates who are in favo[r] of conservation. Take time to write letters to elected official[s] voicing your opinion on important issues.

Most of all, practice self-restraint. By releasing a mini[?]mum of a fish or two per outing, you'll be making a dire[ct] contribution to the environment. Imagine how many fis[h] would survive if all the anglers in your area would release just [a] couple per day! Furthermore, teach children the values o[f] nature and the importance of releasing fish. If they are brough[t] up with this attitude, the new generation might be mor[e] sensitive to the needs of the environment than those of th[e] past. After all, it's their future.

The problems facing our fishery aren't insurmountable. [If] we group together and practice the art of true sportsmanshi[p,] we'll be assured of a productive and stable sport in the comin[g] years.

KNOW YOUR QUARRY

Successful anglers understand the habits and recognize the habitat of their quarry. Every species has its own life style and its own strategy for survival. A fish must concern itself with finding food, avoiding predation, and living long enough to spawn. Accomplishing those primary goals in an ocean or estuary proves to be a demanding task.

Simply by looking at the physical shape of a fish and its tail, one should have a basic concept of the type of territory it will occupy and its feeding behavior. Bottom species are designed to live around some form of structure. They are typically slab-sided with broad, full tails that enable them to weave in and out of rocks, reefs, wrecks, and other bottom configurations. Many ambush their prey or cruise slowly looking for a tasty morsel. Two or three sweeps of the tail drive them forward quickly to catch an escaping meal, but you should also recognize that they won't follow a bait or lure for long distances. That simply isn't their style.

The fastest species such as the tunas and marlins have forked tails that are rigid on the leading edges and softer on the inside. Their bodies are more elongated and swimming motion comes from muscle waves and, in the case of tuna,

The spotted seatrout captures the attention of countless coastal anglers. Live shrimp is still the primary bait, but trout take other natural offerings as well as jigs and plugs.

unbelieveably rapid tail beats. These are open water or pelagic fish shaped to move through the seas easily in a relentless search for food. Flat fish such as the flounder or halibut are destined for a life on the bottom, while elongated creatures typified by the barracuda charge their prey from ambush with lightning speed or ease along in the water column and strike with a suddenness that defies the human eye.

There's always a tradeoff. The faster swimmers often lack maneuverability. A grouper can spin on the proverbial dime and change direction instantly to grab an erratic bait or lure. Tuna and barracuda lack that agility. Once they launch an attack, it's difficult for them to make adjustments. That's why lures targeted for the speed merchants should track as straight as possible without much lateral movement.

A fish's mouth offers insight into its feeding habits. The underslung mouth of the bonefish is termed inferior and indicates that it roots on the bottom. Redfish have a hard nose and similar mouth with eyes set high and forward on the head. Obviously, they are built to root in the bottom in off-color water where visibility is relatively poor. The protruding lower jaw of the tarpon tells us that this species prefers to strike on the same plane or upward, but it will poke around the bottom for tasty tidbits just as a bonefish will pursue some creature at mid-depth.

The surface swirl of a striped bass or bluefish tempts many of us to toss a surface plug at the radiating ripples. Sometimes, the fish will return and crash the offering, but one should remember that the swirl is caused by a movement known as flexed rotation. A fish's backbone prevents it from bending in half. When moving rapidly toward the surface in pursuit of prey or for any other reason, the fish reverses its direction and starts downward by rolling on its side and turning its head toward the bottom. As the tail comes around, it creates the swirl, but the head of the fish is already aimed away from the surface. That's why a weighted artificial that sinks quickly may be a better choice under those conditions.

The observant angler gains an effective edge. He remains alert to everything happening around him and tailors his techniques to the species he seeks. If there are secrets or panaceas for fishing, they have escaped us all these years. Consistent catches usually result from a thorough understanding of one's quarry. There are no shortcuts to success.

HOW FISH SEE

Most predators are visually oriented. Sound or smell may draw them to the scene, but the final attack is usually based on sight. The human eye has an iris or diaphragm that adjusts to the amount of light and eyelids to shade and protect the eyes. Fish have a fixed center aperture and no eyelids. They rely on rod and cone receptors in the eye to handle brightness. Rod receptors are used for night vision and cones generally indicate the ability to see color. For distant vision, we are able to flatten our lenses, but fish rely on a muscle known as the retractor lentis which pulls the whole lens back toward the retina.

From a practical standpoint, a fish's eyes are set on either side of the head and each works independently over an arc of about 180 degrees on each side of the body. There is a narrow overlapping in front where binocular vision occurs and a small blind spot behind the fish. The sharpest vision occurs when an object is at a right angle to one eye. That suggests that a lure or bait may bring a better response when placed alongside one eye rather than directly in front of the fish. The zone of binocular vision aids depth perception, but some fish have difficulty seeing an offering placed right on their noses. Experts believe that a billfish swings from side to side when following a trolled bait to see it better with one eye.

If you've always wondered why fishing can be better early and late in the day, consider the fact that predators gain an advantage in approaching their prey during periods of marginal light. The absence of bright light makes most objects appear in black and white just as it does for humans.

What fish see under various conditions centers on contrast and the background. One type of monofilament line, for example, may be difficult to detect against one background, but easily spotted against another. Angle plays a role. A fish looking up toward the surface sees a silhouette against the sky, while one viewing the same lure laterally gets a different picture. ·

Most fish do see color, but depth and water clarity determine precisely what they will observe. Color is absorbed from the light as it passes through water with the reds and oranges the first to go. Depth and distance produce similar effects. Reds turn to gray within 20 feet and certainly by 30 feet. A red snapper on a reef is not bright red, but a dingy gray. Blues and greens are the last to go, giving the underwater world a cast in those colors. Keep in mind that during dawn and dusk, blues and greens are the most visible colors.

There is no question that under certain conditions, specific colors make a difference in catching fish, but that doesn't happen as often as most folks suspect. A particular color may give an angler confidence in the artificial he is using and that does provide a competitive edge. Except in isolated situations, it pays to ignore subtle color changes and opt for major changes in silhouette. Shift from light to dark or vice versa before worrying about various shades of yellow or green.

The refraction or bending of light rays as they enter the water helps fish to spot you just as easily as you see them. When the water is calm, this periscope effect makes it difficult to approach one's quarry. A ripple on the surface tends to mask the sight of the angler in shallow water. Keeping the sun at your back also helps.

Fish are alert to the slightest movement. Stand perfectly still in the water or aboard a boat and they may swim by blissfully, but move a hand or arm and they react instantly. Under tough conditions, sidearm casts may be more effective than overhand ones where the rod is easily seen. White is extremely visible in terms of clothing, rods, and flylines when fishing shallow water. Even in slightly deeper water, one seldom suspects that he has been seen and the fish alerted.

Students of the sport talk about instance after instance where a fish in shallow water or near the surface spooked when it saw the line or a lure in the air. One must remember that airborne predators are just as deadly to a fish as those in the water.

The striped bass fisherman works hard for his rewards. limited supply of fish and increased regulations make t task of catching a trophy even more difficult.

A NOSE FOR FOOD

In the shadowy, dingy world in which a fish lives, surviv would be difficult if sight were the only sense. Underwa creatures develop a keen sense of smell that can easily dete food or danger with incredible sensitivity. Salmon rely on th ability to discern odors for precise navigation back to the riv and the exact spot of their birth, often traveling hundreds miles in the process.

If you have wondered how a fish can find a piece of b on the bottom, chances are that the sense of smell came in play. Bottom dwellers living in dimly lit waters rely a great de on smell to find food, but most species are affected by sme Minute particles are carried by tide or current and fish have t ability to follow the scent to its source.

Sharks are masters at this and boast a keen directior ability. The zigzag pattern that they follow as they home in o particular smell occurs because they can tell which nost receives the stronger smell and go in that direction until weakens. Then, they shift course in the other direction and forth.

Chumming attracts fish through their sense of smell a observers report that their quarry often comes from a sign cant distance to the source of the odor. That keen olfacto sense in a fish also helps to detect the quality of the food. There are many instances where stale chum does not produce results, while fresh chum in the same waters does.

Smell warns of danger. L-serine given off by humans tends to repel fish. Other odors ranging from gasoline to insect repellent may have a negative effect on fish, although most anglers ignore this aspect. Special products on the market are formulated to either mask or eliminate these extraneous odors so that an angler can touch a bait or lure without leaving negative smell tracks.

A number of other formulations are being sold over the counter guaranteed to attract fish to lures or even natural baits. Many of them seem to work under certain conditions, although one is never certain whether they are tolling in fish or simply eliminating odors of danger. Odor molecules move with the flow of water and that takes a certain amount of time. It is doubtful that a lure sprayed with a scent will be better than one without the attractant on a single cast and retrieve.

What may happen is that the fish follows the lure visually and then picks up the scent just before striking. If you are casting repeatedly in the same spot, the smell track may contribute something.

Strong olfactory senses in fish suggest that bait should be fresh and that we should make every effort to mask human odors. Particularly during periods of low light, a jig tipped with natural bait does a better job than one without. In many situations, a tipped jig outfishes a bare one, demonstrating that smell must be an important factor.

SOUND VERSUS NOISE

Sound travels five times faster in water than it does in air at a rate of about one mile per second. Fish rely on sound to signal the presence of prey or alert them to danger. If you have watched fish for any period, you know that they instinctively flee from unfamiliar sounds, always moving away from the source.

Large predators sometimes invade a chum slick simply because they respond to the sound of smaller fish feeding. They can actually hear potential prey as it devours the free meal. Simultaneous feeding by several fish will also trigger others into starting to feed. Consider it a chain reaction, but it happens frequently. In that same chumming scene, the sound of a few school members finding the chum and feasting on it attracts others.

Gamesters are intensely aware of the distress vibrations given off by injured or impaired fish. A struggling forage fish on the surface will be engulfed quickly by any nearby predator. That's why you can fish a live bait around a school of the same species of baitfish and your bait will be hit. One might think that it would be chance alone, but the distress vibrations given off by the tethered bait telegraph the position of an easy meal. The more the bait struggles and splashes, the greater the effect it will have. That's why a hooked fish is sometimes attacked near the boat by a larger predator drawn to the scene by the sounds of the distressed fish.

Unique in the animal kingdom, the lateral line on either side of a fish is an extremely precise, sound-detecting organ. It responds to low frequency sound within relatively short range in a system known as near field displacement. Anything moving through the water disturbs the molecules and this is detected by neuromasts in the fish's body. The accuracy of the system borders on the amazing, enabling a fish to strike prey it cannot see with repeated success. The lateral line makes it possible for a prowling striped bass to grab a black eel on a particularly dark night.

If you look closely at the sides of any fish, you can see the lateral line. On the snook, it appears as a black stripe over a silvery body and is extremely pronounced. Fish feeding frantically in a chum slick dash and dart back and forth without ever crashing into a schoolmate. Two or more fish approaching the same bait from different directions never have a head-on collision. Scientists suspect that lateral line sensitivity enables these frenzied feeders to avoid each other. They also believe that near field displacement helps in schooling behavior, allowing each fish to maintain its relative position with others in the school. When the shoal of fish changes direction, no member continues on a straight course. A flanking movement occurs in which every individual turns at the same time in the identical direction.

There are negative sounds. A plug landing too close to an oversized shark or a 100-pound tarpon in shallow water will frighten the giant. Noise from an outboard cranking or running over fish may spook the very fish one plans to catch. Any low frequency noise aboard a boat such as sliding a tackle box

During spring and fall, big channel bass prowl the surf and respond to artificial lures as well as natural baits. They are tough brawlers in the suds, making victory that much sweeter.

on deck, dropping a pair of pliers, or the thud of a misplaced foot could chase your quarry or at least alert it to danger. Silence on the water has its benefits inshore or offshore.

USE A THERMOMETER

Biologists consider temperature to be the single most important factor governing the occurrence and behavior of fish. Each species has its own temperature preferences and limits. They cannot survive very long beyond those limits and continuously seek temperatures within their comfort zones.

The life processes of a fish speed up as the water approaches the upper temperature range for the species and slow down in the lower range. It takes longer to digest food in cooler water and fish probably won't feed as frequently since all of the body functions tend to slow.

Many fish are so aware of temperature that they can sense changes as insignificant as a fraction of a degree. Water that is only one or two degrees cooler or warmer than surrounding areas may suddenly become a hot spot for fish. A thermometer is an invaluable tool for monitoring changes in water temperature and should be used regularly. Don't discount the importance of minor changes.

In cold water, fish become sluggish. They may refuse to chase a bait or lure any distance and could easily ignore anything that moved particularly fast. Under those conditions, topwater offerings probably would be ignored. Water temperatures determine the body temperatures of your quarry and when the mercury plummets, the fish's functions have slowed considerably.

Take the time to learn the temperature preferences and limits for the species you intend to catch. During marginal times of the year, you could save a lot of time by not fishing waters that fall outside the limits. If you know the species of forage fish most prevalent in the area, check on their temperature limits. When the schools of baitfish move to warmer or cooler waters, you can be reasonably certain the predators

will go right with them.

Bluewater trollers have learned that warm gyres or eddies branching off from a main current could hold fish while surrounding waters do not. Cold water intrusions sometimes put an instant damper on the fishing and many area anglers fail to realize why their favorite species turned off without warning.

Shallow waters heat up more quickly and cool down faster than the deeper seas around them. On the flats, water temperature can be critical in locating your quarry. Either extreme presents problems. Tarpon, for example, wait for the water to reach 75 degrees before they venture into the shallows. They won't be there when it is 73 degrees and only a handful of fish will brave 74 degree water, but when the temperature hits the magic number, here come the silver kings. How they know defies comprehension, but it happens with regularity.

A FEW MORE THOUGHTS

Fishermen are frequently guilty of what scientists call anthropomorphism. It's nothing more serious than giving fish and animals human characteristics. We expect them to behave and react much as we would do. Fish are basically creatures of habit. No matter where in the world you catch a specific species, it's behavior patterns are similar right down to the battle it wages once it is hooked.

All of us have a tendency to overcomplicate fishing and fishing techniques. Our quarry focuses on nothing more than feeding, escaping predation, and hanging around to spawn and continue the species. An understanding of these goals and the methods employed to reach them result in more meaningful catches. Those who consistently score well are keen observers of what takes place on the water. Rather than trying to force a fish to accept what they offer, they change approaches continuously until they discover what the fish is willing to accept. It's a system that works.

White marlin become more suspicious of any tension on the line during the dropback than other species of billfish. When baiting a white, maintain the minimum thumb pressure possible to avoid an overrun.

THE TACKLE SYSTEM

Selecting the right tackle shares the spotlight with mastering productive fishing techniques. Each becomes a vital component of the total experience and each plays a critical role in the pleasure and satisfaction that accrues from the sport. A skilled carpenter may be able to work miracles with a few basic hand tools, but think of what his hands and mind can construct once he is armed with the appropriate equipment.

All tackle represents a compromise. There are no universal rods, reels, or lines that perform to perfection across the board on every marine assignment. Many will serve well in a variety of situations, but there are always limitations. Beginners start with a single outfit and soon feel the need for additional gear. It's surprising how quickly an enthusiastic angler enlarges his arsenal to meet the challenges of different species and conditions.

Purchasing the proper tackle begins with the systems concept. Rod, reel, and line must work as a team to provide the maximum benefit. Whatever you select should fit into the total picture through careful planning even if you buy one thing at a time. Individual items acquired at random without giving thought to the system tend to be mismatched. Before you shop, analyze your needs. Utilize the advice of more experienced anglers where you are uncertain, but remember that the final choice should be yours since you have to fish with whatever you pick.

Perhaps the best way to assemble the right combination focuses on thinking backwards. The usual approach centers on getting the rod first, adding the reel, and then spooling the line on the reel. It makes more sense to start with the line. You don't have to buy it initially, but you should select it. Once you know the breaking strength of the line you plan to use, your task comes down to finding a rod tailored to handle line of that pound test and a reel with adequate capacity to hold the line.

If spinning is your game and you want to use 12-pound test monofilament, then you need a rod with the taper to cast that line and the backbone to fight a fish on 12-pound. The

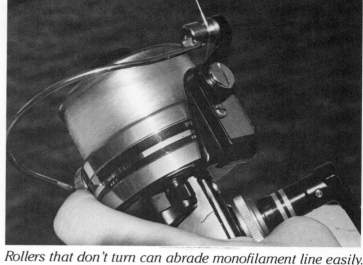

Rollers that don't turn can abrade monofilament line easily. Make sure this vital part receives periodic lubrication.

bottom fisherman who decides on 20-pound test should have no trouble assembling the system. Light line married to a heavy rod doesn't work and vice versa. That's why it is so important to decide first on the breaking strength of the line.

RODS

The rod lies at the heart of the tackle system. Countless production models in every price range flood the marketplace and there is always the appeal of a custom built stick complete with your name on the blank. Regardless of design or manufacture, the rod must present the bait or lure to the fish, set the hook, do battle, and perform well with the breaking strength of the line you decide to use. Rank these factors in order of importance for a particular situation. If you intend to land an oversized denizen on relatively light gear, you may want to concentrate on the fighting characteristics of the rod rather

When line gets low on a spinning spool, it's time to replace it. There was enough on this reel to handle the seatrout, but a trophy fish surely would have been a problem.

Plug outfits are excellent fish-fighting tools and fun to use. Revolving spool reels are gaining in popularity among light tackle anglers.

than the casting performance. When presentation outweighs the problems of the subsequent fight, make that your primary concern in choosing a rod.

It's marvelous that an army of anglers can invade tackle shops across the land, pick rods off the racks, wave them around like cavalry sabers, and declare how great they feel. More knowledgeable fishermen remain skeptical, preferring a series of tests to determine suitability. Start by studying the components of the rod in terms of quality and workmanship. With the exception of stand up, offshore rods which have more, the rod you select should have a minimum of five guides plus a tiptop if it is 7-feet long or under. Longer rods should have more guides.

When you are considering a casting rod, ask the clerk if you can put a reel on the rod and actually try it behind the shop or in a nearby area. Carry your own reel, if necessary, and take along a casting plug or a lure without hooks. You'll know in a hurry whether or not it does the job. With the newer materials, it becomes extremely difficult to tell much about a rod without trying it.

To test the fighting power, put your reel on the rod, rig the line through the guides, and have the clerk hold the end of the line while you apply pressure to the rod. Make sure there are enough guides to lead the line along the curvature of the blank. If the line touches the blank at any point or the radius of each bend over a guide is too severe, look for another rod.

Regardless of material, the majority of rod blanks feature tubular construction in which cloth of a given fiber is wrapped around a mandril, coated with resin or a bonding agent, and then heated in an oven. There are still a few rods made from solid fiberglass available at the low end, but a tubular model generally rates as a better choice.

From a practical standpoint, rod materials include E-glass, S-glass, graphite, and composites. E-glass is the original fiberglass and it is still used widely because it is an exceptionally tough and strong material that proves very forgiving. S-glass represents a second generation in fiberglass construction, boasting much lighter weight, a bit more sensitivity, and good casting characteristics at a price below graphite.

Modulus of elasticity or simply modulus refers to the stiffness of a material or its resistance to deflection. The stiffer the material, the more sensitive it is to vibrations. First generation graphite is about three times stiffer than fiberglass and twice as strong. Graphite fibers only elongate about one percent before they fail, while the workhorse E-glass elongates about four percent. That's why fiberglass is so forgiving. However, graphite has come a long way and we are actually into its second generation. Newer graphite rods have become much more forgiving, increasingly sensitive, and even lighter in weight than the original entries. Prices have also dropped dramatically.

The action of a rod describes the taper of the blank. Fast action blanks flex near the tip, medium action flexes about half way down the shaft, and slow action works closer to the butt. Rod buyers sometimes confuse action with power. Power really represents the blank's stiffness in relative terms. The same action or taper can be produced with different levels of power. To fight a fish effectively, you must have adequate

reserve power in a rod. Too little power causes the blank to collapse under the pressure of a fish.

When load is applied to a blank, the tip starts to bend toward the force. The strain starts to shift down the blank toward the handle. As increased pressure is applied, the load continues to shift farther toward the butt. Unless there is reserve power in this area of a blank, it becomes increasingly difficult to pump a fish. Serious anglers opt for rods that have an excess of reserve power, even with relatively light lines. If you can't move the fish, you can't land it regardless of the tackle.

The hundreds of fishing rod designs can be reduced to six basic types. Spinning is by far the most popular, because it is easy to use and casts without backlash. The typical spinning rod spans 6' to 7' and is available in a number of action and power combinations. Plug or bait casting rods range from 5 to 7' in length, with the longer ones better suited to marine angling. Along the Gulf Coast, the popping rod is a specialized model of the plug rod. With the sophistication in modern bait casting reels including magnetic casting control, plug tackle has enjoyed increasing popularity in recent years and more of it will find its way into salt water.

Surf rods may be built for spinning or conventional reels. At one time, an 11-footer was considered long, but rods made from graphite stretch to 13' or longer. On the short side, jetty jockeys may use an 8' or 9' stick. There is no question that graphite adds distance to the cast and makes the extra long rods feasible. You'll also find some excellent designs crafted from S-glass which is light and rugged.

The so-called boat rods are targeted toward conventional reels and tailored primarily for bottom fishing or very light trolling. Most of these are popularly priced for the beginning angler, but their value is really questionable. One would be better off aboard a party boat or on a pier or bridge with a slightly longer rod such as an 8' surf stick or even a husky 7' spinning rod used with a conventional reel. There is no hard rule that says you have to use a spinning reel on a spinning rod. In fact, you can always have new conventional guides wrapped on the same blank.

Trolling rods are rated by the breaking strength of the line they are designed to handle. The standard sizes include 1

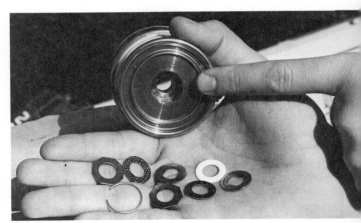

Smooth drags are essential for consistently landing fish. Most systems rely on free-floating, soft washers between hard washers that are keyed to the shaft or the spool.

pound, 20, 30, 50, 80, and 130. Quality rods feature roller guides, machined reel seats, and aluminum butts. The point to remember is that there are no standards. A 30 pound rod from one manufacturer may be heavier or lighter than that of another maker. It pays to compare and pick the model that has the backbone and components you need.

Anglers aboard the California long range boats have been using shorter, stand up rods for years to battle big fish from the decks of the party packets. A well-engineered stand up rod does wonders when you belly up to the covering board, providing you know how to use it. This style has gained tremendous popularity on all coasts, but it does have limitations. Remember that it is geared for stand up fishing. If you are going to use a chair, a regular trolling rod may be better. The stand ups have more guides and a special taper to facilitate pumping. Experts are reasonably convinced that roller guides on these rods are a better choice than standard fixed foot guides.

Finally, the age old question of whether to buy a one-piece or two-piece rod lingers. There was a time when ferruling took some of the action out of a blank, but the latest manufacturing techniques make it difficult to tell the difference between a one-piece and two-piece model. In fact, some multi-ferruled rods perform amazingly well.

REELS

Reels could be called the pivotal point in the tackle system, because they should match the rod and the line. If the reel is too small or too large to balance the other components, it becomes cumbersome to use. Line capacity and drag performance rank as the primary functions. Castability follows closely for those models designed to handle that task. Price should never be accepted as the sole test for quality. It

Serious stand up fishing requires quality tackle including a rod specifically designed for the task, a quality reel, well-made gimbal belt and harness, plus non-slip footwear.

may well be an indicator, but it is never a guarantee.

Competition fosters innovation. The marketplace currently contains an impressive offering of reels for every type of fishing imaginable and in a multitude of sizes. The majority of these reels perform exceptionally well and boast a variety of features that were not available a few years ago.

Whenever you decide to buy a reel, it should be the right one for a rod you already own or one you plan to purchase. That's the way the system concept works. No matter how perfectly a reel operates, it isn't worthwhile unless you can match it to the right rod and line.

Every manufacturer has its own designations and numbering systems for its reels. The only sensible approach at the moment centers on big game trolling reels where some makers finally listened and began calling them 30-pound reels, 50-pound reels, and so forth to match the breaking strength of the line and the rating on the trolling rod. With other types of reels, you have to check the literature or the information on the box to determine line capacity. The maker of a 30-pound reel is really telling you that the product holds an adequate amount of 30-pound test line and has a drag system tailored to fishing with 30-pound test line.

Perhaps the day will come when manufacturers take the same approach with spinning, bait casting, and other conventional reels. That way, if you plan to use 10-pound test line, you can buy a reel rated for that breaking strength and you'll know that it has the capacity and drag system for 10-pound test. Until then, you'll have to check the various sizes and pick the right one for the fishing you plan to do.

In choosing a reel, focus on line capacity first. Ask yourself if it will hold enough line of the required breaking strength to handle the species you expect to catch. The angler who stalks bonefish on a tropical flat will need a lot more 8-pound or 10-pound test on a reel than someone trying for school bluefish in a chum slick.

As a general rule, you should have a minimum of 150 yards of line on a light reel and preferably 200 yards to 300 yards or more. On the offshore grounds with trolling tackle, figure the minimum around 350 yards to 400 yards. Even if the reel isn't stripped on the first run or the second, the actual length of line retrieved for each revolution of the handle drops

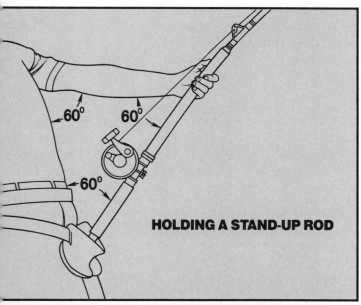

HOLDING A STAND-UP ROD

To get maximum performance from a stand-up rod, position is critical. The gimbal belt is worn low and over the groin area with the pads against the thigh muscles. Reach forward with your left hand and grasp the foregrip as high as you can, while remaining comfortable. Note the equal angles formed between the body, arm, and rod.

dramatically when spool diameter decreases drastically.

It really makes sense to insist on adequate capacity to handle long running fish regardless of what you plan to hook. That way, if a trophy comes along or you tangle with an unexpected species, you won't run short of line.

Instead of viewing the drag on a reel as a brake, think of it as a resistance to rotation. A brake is designed to stop something; a drag is tailored to slow the spool by applying predetermined pressure. When the drag binds temporarily or backs off by itself, you're going to lose fish. Quality drags feature a full range of adjustments with plenty of room to fine tune the exact amount of pressure. If the drag goes from free spool to full in a half turn of the knob, wheel, or lever, you are going to be handicapped by the inability to establish a precise setting.

The amount of drag surface plus the size and type of the washers are important. You want as much surface as you can get, remembering that larger washers are better than smaller ones. Most reels alternate soft and hard washers with the hard washers keyed so that they do not rotate. Multi-stage drags are often superior to single stage drags, but there are exceptions. You'll probably find some type of spring pressing against the series of washers. This helps to equalize the pressure and eliminate vibrations.

If you already own the rod for which the new reel is intended, take it along. Before you settle on a specific model, put the reel on the rod and see how it feels. Make certain it is comfortable to use and that it is not dwarfed by the rod or overpowers the rod. Span a spinning reel with your hand and check that your forefinger can reach the bail to pick up the line. With a baitcasting mill, does it feel right when you cradle the reel and turn the handle or try to put the reel in free spool for a cast?

More spinning reels are sold than other types. For salt water work, stick with open-faced spinning rather than closed-face or spin casting. Open the bail and turn the handle to check the ease with which the bail closes. If possible, you want a reel that allows you to also close the bail manually without having to turn the handle. Look at the roller on the bail and make certain it will turn under pressure. Get a feel of the handle knob and see if it is comfortable.

There are definite limitations. Spinning spools under two inches in diameter are not intended for lines heavier than about 10-pound test and even that may be heavy. Twenty pound test line represents the upper limits of spinning. Some anglers spool heavier line, but they sacrifice performance. If you have to fish more than 20-pound test, use conventional tackle. Above all, you want reliability in a reel. Settle on the product of a major manufacturer who readily stands behind its reels and who has a good track record.

Improvements in bait casting reels over the years are legendary. Magnetic casting control virtually eliminates the backlash problem when set correctly and many now have excellent drag systems. Certain conventional reels boast the same features with increased line capacity and drags that can handle heavier lines.

Relatively inexpensive conventional reels, many with levelwinds, accommodate the basic needs of the generalist. They perform well for bottom fishing, chumming, light trolling,

For casting accuracy, use two hands and bring the roc straight back toward your nose. If your eyes are locked on the target, your cast will be, too.

and other assignments. Most rely on a star wheel for setting the drag, but the trend is toward a lever drag on some models.

Reels made primarily for trolling fall into two basic categories: the top-of-the-line class reels with lever drags and the popularly priced workhorses which may have a star wheel or a lever drag. It's difficult to make a poor choice if you rely on the leading brands. Both levels will perform well. The differences parallel a car for transportation versus a luxury model. They'll both get you there, but you'll enjoy that luxury car a lot more.

A number of offshore reels are still designated by the "O" for ocean. To remember the sizes, start with 30-pound class which matches a 4/0. As the line size increases, the reel size gets larger. A 6/0 is right for 50-pound; a 9/0 for 80, and so forth. To accommodate people who want to fight giant fish and need more line capacity, some of the top trolling reels are made in wide spool as well as standard spool models and the larger ones may even offer two gear ratios.

Gear ratios reflect how many times the spool rotates for one complete revolution of the handle. A lower gear ratio generates more power, but recovers line more slowly. The trend in smaller reels is toward faster gear ratios. Spinning and bait casting reels are now available with gear ratios of 5:1 and more. That means that the spool turns five times when the handle makes a single revolution.

ckle should be tailored to the task. The beginning angler should use heavier gear until he develops the skill to battle a fish ith authority on lighter lines.

LINES

There is no such thing as a second chance when fighting fish. If the thin web of monofilament or Dacron parts, you an add another story about the fish that got away to your ollection of anecdotes. Anything short of premium line roves to be false economy in the long run. They reflect better uality control, the ability to maintain uniformity, and more gid standards; that's why they cost more.

The latest technology enables line manufacturers to educe the diameter of monofilament and still maintain the rength. This gives the angler the option of putting more line f a given test on the reel or enjoying the same capacity with a ightly heavier line. Diameter holds the key to capacity and astability. A thinner line tends to cast better and it seems to nprove the presentation of bait or lure.

Monofilament has a definite life span and should be placed regularly. The ultra-violet rays of the sun and exces- ve heat destroy a line rapidly. Abrasion caused by the line nning over some obstruction, a rough roller on a spinning el, or faulty guide seriously weakens the line. You can feel rasion by running your fingers over the line. Spools, of urse, should be filled to capacity and line added or the hole line replaced when the quantity drops a noticeable nount. Fishing with half a spool of line saps drag perfor- ance and leads to lost fish.

Newcomers often ask why many lines test more than the ated breaking strength on the label. The law specifies that e line may not test less than the stated breaking strength, but does not give any guidance beyond that. It's perfectly legal to label 14-pound test or even 20-pound test as 10-pound. The exception occurs with labeling for tournament line in which the product is guaranteed to break under the stated test. The problem here is that no one knows how much under. You would want 10 pound to break consistently at 9.9 pounds or something close to that. If it were labeled tournament line, it could break at 6 pounds and meet the legal requirements.

Monofilament is much more forgiving than Dacron because of the stretch factor. Dacron will elongate under 10 percent, but mono may have more than 25 percent stretch. A relative handful of offshore anglers rely on Dacron and partic- ularly those trying to pump big fish up from the depths. Most fishing, however, is done with monofilament and it is important to recognize that all mono is not the same. Each formulation represents a balance of properties and, obviously, a compro- mise. These are determined in the manufacture of the line. As an example, anglers often believe that stiffer monofilament is more abrasion resistant. Actually, abrasion resistance is built into the line and is not a function of stiffness or limpness.

All line is visible to fish underwater. How it shows up depends on its color compared to a specific background and the angle from which it is viewed. Fluorescent lines, however, are much easier to see underwater than any standard colora- tion. Once you've looked at them yourself, chances are that you will opt for clear line or any of the basic colors.

The entire tackle system focuses on the breaking strength of the line. That's what really determines the type of rod and reel you will need to complete the outfit. Start with the line and the pieces of the puzzle should fall in place easier.

THE SEVEN-STEP BIMINI

STEP 1

Start with about six feet of line and double the tag end back against the standing part to form a loop. Hold both the tag end and standing part firmly with the left hand, while you slip the four fingers of your right hand in the loop. Keep the loop fairly tight by separating your hands. Then, rotate your right hand twenty times in a clockwise direction, twisting one strand of line around the other.

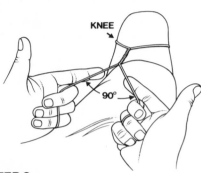

STEP 2

Prop your right foot on a tackle box, chair, cooler, etc. that will cause the knee to flex and bend. Slip the loop still held in your right hand over the bent knee. Keep the line tight so the twists cannot unravel. Separate the standing part of the line (left hand) from the tag end (right hand) so that they form a 90° angle. Pull the tag end and standing part toward you evenly, maintaining tension and a 90° angle. The twists will tighten and move toward the knee.

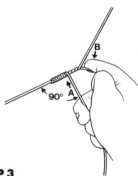

STEP 3

Once the twists are tight, shift the position of both hands to the right, retaining the 90° angle. The standing part is in line with the twists and the tag end is at right angles to them. As you pull on the standing part with your left hand, the tag end in your right hand will start to feed over the twists. Maintain moderate tension, but allow the line to feed (A). The forefinger of your right hand placed in the loop and pulled toward you will help the tag end to feed smoothly.

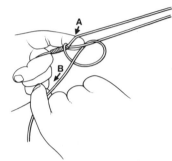

STEP 4

When the wraps over the twists reach the junction of the loop (which is still over your knee), hold them in place (A) by pushing against the twists with the forefinger of your left hand. Make a single half-hitch with the tag end around the right leg of the loop and pull the tag end (B) until the half-hitch seats. You no longer have to maintain tension and may remove the loop from your knee.

STEP 5

To finish the knot with a locking hitch, hold both legs of the loop together with your right hand or slip the loop over any projection. Lay the tag end against both legs, leaving enough slack underneath to form a semi-circle. Wrap the tag end around both legs of the loop five times, passing each turn inside the semi-circle. You are working back toward the twist. Moisten the wraps and pull the tag end slowly.

STEP 6

As you pull the tag end (arrow) slowly, the locking hitch continues to form. You may have to use the thumb and forefinger of your right hand to draw the wraps back as you tighten so that they don't jump over the knot.

STEP 7

Draw the locking hitch down as tightly as you can (use pliers if necessary) and trim the tag end close to the knot. You just tied a Bimini Twist.

THE BUSINESS END

Terminal tackle holds the key to catching fish. Subtleties in choosing and rigging hooks, sinkers, swivels, and leaders account for a significant difference in results. Too many anglers tend to discount or ignore the importance of selecting the right terminal gear for a given situation, preferring to rig with whatever happens to be at hand. Successful fishermen refuse to compromise on this aspect, pointing out that its the only part of the total outfit that the fish actually see and to which they must respond.

The size of a hook, weight of a sinker, strength of a swivel, and diameter of the leader determine the effectiveness of the presentation. Each component must be matched to the species, habitat, and the rod, reel, and line. Minor variations create major problems on those marginal days when feeding frenzies are scarce and fish become increasingly selective. If an offering doesn't look natural and appealing, it will be refused.

HOOKS

Fashioned from a piece of wire, the fish hook appears to be a simple device designed to penetrate the jaw of a fish and remain there through the battle. It traces its history back to the early days of mankind, but modern versions feature sophisticated and complex engineering concepts that often elude the casual inspector. There are thousands of styles and countless sizes in use today, but little standardization among the world's manufacturers. Actual sizes vary by style and by fabricator, so it is difficult to find identical patterns and matching hooks from two makers.

Even the numbering system is archaic. As the number decreases toward one, the hooks increase in size (in most instances). A number two hook is larger than a number six. After size one, just the reverse is true. Hooks add a /0 after the number such as 1/0, 2/0, 3/0, and up. A 4/0 hook is much bigger than a 2/0 hook and a 1/0 surpasses a one.

From a practical standpoint, an angler should focus on the important aspects of hook selection. Too much emphasis

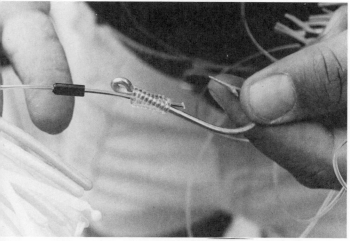

A crimp or small egg sinker secured to the leader right above the hook in a trolling lure takes the strain and prevents the hook from jackknifing when you set it on a fish.

Use a loop knot to tie a bucktail. It allows the lure to work more effectively at a designed angle.

can be placed on type of eye, whether or not a hook is offset, and dozens of other factors. There is no universal hook, but you can certainly fish around the world with only a modest selection of styles and sizes. Short-shank tuna hooks along with the extremely popular O'Shaughnessy pattern will cover a variety of assignments. Flounder fishermen opt for fine wire, long shank hooks. Offshore enthusiasts have their own guidelines for hooks. There are always differences of opinion, but the starting point lies with hooks that fit the bait or lure being used and the species one expects to catch.

Perhaps the most critical aspects involve wire diameter and hook size. As a basic rule, the finer the diameter of the wire from which the hook is made, the easier it is to set that hook. Smaller sizes tend to penetrate more easily than larger ones and hooks with shorter and less pronounced barbs offer better penetration. You can drive a fine wire, barbless hook through the toughest mouths if it is sharp.

Wire diameter and hook size should be matched against the breaking strength of the line. The lighter the line, the finer the diameter and the smaller the size of the hook. Trying to plant a husky hook in the hard mouth of a marine creature with light line goes beyond a challenge. Consider it extremely difficult at best. The converse also causes problems. You can exert enough pressure with heavy tackle to straighten light wire hooks. As long as the hook is matched to the line, you can take on some pretty big critters with relatively small hooks.

Few fishermen ever ask for hooks by manufacturer, model number, and size. Instead, they ballpark their request and rely on the clerk to supply the popular styles and sizes. Stand in a tackle shop and you'll hear customers say, "Gimme some bluefish hooks" or "What kind of hooks do I need for summer flounder?" The person behind the counter seldom matches hook sizes to the tackle, preferring to merely dish out the standard fare. All of us have the tendency to fish larger hooks than necessary and, in the process, we make it tougher to drive the barb home.

With live bait, the size and weight of the hook affects how well the forage fish will swim. Too heavy a hook will tire a bait quickly and it becomes less effective. Even with dead bait or cut bait, the hook should fit the offering neatly and remain somewhat concealed. Size and bite play important roles here. Match the hook to the bait as well as the line. Finding the right combination makes a difference.

Practicing conservation on the water and releasing unneeded fish is rapidly becoming a necessity if populations are to be maintained. Increased fishing pressure and more sophisticated techniques take their toll on existing stocks. For that reason, many anglers are switching to bronze hooks or hooks made from metals that will rust more easily than stainless steel. If a fish is hooked deep, one need only cut the leader close to the mouth and the hook will eventually rust out. Non-stainless hooks simply rust more quickly and that's better for the fish.

THE RIGHT LEADER

A leader is a length of heavier material between the end of the fishing line and the terminal tackle. In a practical sense, this vital link serves as a buffer against abrasion and protection against a fish's dentures. Somewhat erroneously, it is often referred to as a shock leader when its true function lies in

The time taken to sharpen a hook will pay dividends in terms of fish caught. Dull hooks spawn stories about the one that got away.

resisting chafing or cutting. Surf casters usually employ tru shock leaders when they attach a length of heavier monofil ment longer than the rod. This larger diameter mono takes th "shock" of the cast as the rod is whipped forward and keep the lighter fishing line from breaking.

If you remember three basic rules about leaders, you gain an edge over the average angler who usually ties mono wire on the end of the line without giving it much though Rule 1: Whenever possible, use monofilament leader materi in preference to single strand wire, coated wire, cable, anything else. Rule 2: Regardless of the leader material, sele the finest diameter that will do the job. Rule 3: Make th overall leader as short as practical consistent with the situatic and objectives.

Let's take a more detailed look at those rules and why the make a difference. The trend today points toward monofi ment leaders over any other material and for good reaso Experience continues to show that monofilament consistent produces more strikes than wire or cable. That doesn't mea that you won't catch fish with metal or plastic coated leade but over the long haul, mono outfishes metal.

If you chum bluefish along the Atlantic coast, you discover that you get more strikes in the slick with 60-pour test mono than with wire of the same strength. The sam results apply to the rapier-billed sailfish. Rely on mono ar you'll get more strikes. Of course, everything in fishing is tradeoff. With the sharp-toothed bluefish, you run the risk being cut off, but the number of pickups with mono over wi makes it worthwhile.

There was a time when blue water trollers rigged artifici lures with 49-strand aircraft cable or tethered live bait targete for marlin the size of freight cars to this heavy braid. Aircra cable may be a necessity for sharks with dentures like me cleavers, but marlin fishermen are opting for heavy monofi ment with the hooks either snelled or crimped. Even tho who tow expensive lures around the oceans of the world fir that they don't experience very many cutoffs with monofi ment.

Some fishermen erroneously believe that stiffer mon filament is more abrasion resistant. Actually, stiffness has litt to do with mono's ability to withstand scuffing and chafir Abrasion resistance is a property built into the monofilame during manufacturing. Any mono combines a balance properties in what can best be described as a tradeoff. If th maker focuses on certain facets, others are diminished. Whe you find leader material with good abrasion resistance, sti with it.

For critters such as sharks, barracuda, king mackere wahoo, and others with mouths full of razor blades, yc should resort to wire leader. Single strand stainless is th logical choice, but you may want to use plastic coate braided wire because it is softer and more pliable. From a fis catching standpoint, many veterans rely on single stran citing more strikes as their primary reason.

The age old argument of bright wire versus brown coffee colored continues to exist. Fish see all leader materi but some blends in better than others. That depends on th amount of light and the background against which it is viewe In certain situations, bright wire may be less visible and

*ilm canisters make ideal containers for hooks. Label the
ops with style and size and place the canisters in a plastic
ox. It's a worthwhile system.*

ther cases, coffee color serves as a mask. The final decision
yours.

Unlike mono which can be knotted easily in a variety of
ays, single strand wire must be twisted. It is important to
ote that you <u>never</u> snip off the tag end of wire with cutting
liers. The correct technique is to bend and break the tag end
so that the burr does not stick out. If you've ever grabbed a
ire leader with a sharp piece of wire projecting from the
vist, you'll have plenty of time to think about it while the slice
your hand heals.

Coated wire can be knotted with some basic ties and it
an also be superficially twisted and fused together with the
eat from a match. Cable must be secured with crimped
eeves. This same method is also used on very heavy mono-
lament that is too stiff to tie or seat a knot by pulling tight.

Leader diameter does make a difference over a period of
me. Those who fish for tuna, albacore, and bonito in chum
icks know how leader shy these critters can get. There are
ays when experts go to lighter and lighter leaders before they
re able to put a bend in the rod from the weight of a fish on the
ther end. The same rule applies to wire, cable, or any other
aterial. Pick the finest diameter that will do the job and stick
ith it. If 50-pound test is adequate, 80-pound is not neces-
irily better. It could be a handicap.

Finally, be aware of leader length. The shorter the leader
rithin practical limits, the better. Going back to our bluefish
xample, if you find it necessary to use wire as protection
gainst the chopper's teeth, use 4" to 6." That's all you need to
ounter the teeth and the remainder of the leader can be
ade from monofilament. The same theory applies to any
oothy denizen. There is no reason why you cannot combine
ire and monofilament by using a tiny barrel swivel or by tying
e mono directly to the wire using an Albright knot.

When casting spinning or plug gear, short leaders that
ang below the tiptop eliminate the problem of knots going
rough the guides. With some species, it pays to use a short
ace of heavy leader material next to the hook or lure and
then back that up with a lighter leader that may stretch across
the body of the fish during the battle.

Offshore trollers use longer leaders because of the length
of the fish. A mate would have difficulty grabbing the monofilament or wire on a big fish if the leader were too short.
There is an equally strong argument against long leaders in
blue water, particularly when fishing aboard a smaller boat.
With a short leader, the angler can actually fight the fish to
boatside using the rod and reel. If the swivel hits the tiptop in
front of a 15' or 20' leader, you have the problem of pulling the
fish alongside by hand.

For those who must handle long leaders attached to big
fish, a pair of cotton gloves will help to protect the hands.
There are also gloves made from synthetic fibers that are
excellent. If you are going to play with wire or cable, you
might want gloves made from leather.

AS THE SWIVEL TURNS

A swivel is nothing more than a primitive thrust bearing
designed to handle a rotational force called torque and prevent twist in the fishing line. At the same time, it must cope
with a straight pull or load caused by pressure on the fishing
line as the bait, lure, or a fish on the other end moves through
the water. Although swivels are relatively inexpensive, this is
not the place to save a few pennies with low-priced imports.
When bearing surfaces are not smooth and correctly engi-
neered, linear load may keep the swivel from turning, creating
instant line twist.

As a rule of thumb, use the smallest size swivel that will do
the job. For complex reasons, smaller swivels sometimes
rotate better than larger ones and are better suited to handle
the load. At the same time, experienced fishermen minimize
the size of terminal gear, because they feel that it contributes
more toward proper presentation of bait or lure.

In somewhat of an oversimplification, the most common
swivels are the twisted eye barrel, split eye barrel, bead chain,
and the ball bearing. You can recognize the twisted eye or
single head barrel by looking at the wire eye on each side. The
wire is twisted around itself to form the eye. Consider these to
be of poor quality with questionable strength and performance. They are no longer manufactured in the United States,
but imported in significant quantity.

The split eye barrel forms a loop or eye on either side with
a piece of wire that comes from under the barrel, makes a
circle, and returns to the barrel. As a group, these are better
than the twisted eye, although there are several qualities of
split head barrels. The best advice anyone can give you in
buying swivels is to insist on brand names that you know and
respect. Quality companies make quality products. It's that
simple.

Bead chains are often attached to trolling sinkers and
used in certain types of rigs. They are reasonably strong and
have a great deal of flexibility that tends to keep them on
center. In the tradeoff, bead chain is longer than a barrel
swivel and often requires a bit more care to avoid corrosion or
pitting.

Ball bearing swivels represent the ultimate, because they
are much more efficient than the slider types. Basically, there
is a great deal less friction when something rolls than when it

slides against another surface. Not all ball bearing swivels are the same, so it pays to buy those offered by leading companies. They are used primarily in offshore trolling, but smaller sizes work very well with spinning tackle or with lures that tend to put a twist in the line.

Three way swivels are designed to produce three separate leads for a sinker, main line, and leader in bottom fishing. Most of them are not very strong, but then they weren't designed for battling big fish. If you fish the bottom, use the smallest swivels and terminal gear practical. The more hardware you have, the less delicate the presentation. Spreaders and other forms of shaped metal with swivels, snaps, and other items hanging from them are cumbersome at best. They may catch their share of fish, but tend to be the tool of the uninformed beginner rather than the choice of the veteran.

In many casting setups and in some bottom fishing assignments, swivels are not used. Instead, the terminal gear is tied directly to the line or leader material is knotted to the line. The caster enjoys the luxury of reeling the leader through the tiptop and into the guides, providing the knot is small and neat. With a swivel, there is often a restriction at the tiptop.

When line twist becomes a problem, a quality swivel helps to eliminate it. With some lures that have a tendency to spin, two small swivels may prove better than a single larger one. Where you locate the swivel is also important. To avoid line twist, at least one swivel must be between the terminal gear and the line. If you want to protect the leader, a swivel should be on the terminal side of any stabilizing device such as a trolling sinker as well.

A number of swivels are made with snaps attached to one end. These might make sense when attaching a sinker or for trolling, but snap swivels prove to be a handicap when attaching hooks or lures directly to them. The snap in a trolling situation allows you to change lures, baits, and sinkers quickly when they are attached to leaders with loops or swivels at the end. You simply open the snap, remove one offering, and slip the loop of another rig right on the snap.

Cutting corners on swivels is false economy. When you need a swivel, use the best you can buy. Line twist isn't easy to remove and serious line twist may force you to replace the monofilament or Dacron. To remove line twist, cut off all terminal tackle including the swivel and drag the line behind a moving boat for a few minutes. If this doesn't take the twist out, you have problems and will have to replace the line.

A WEIGHTY SUBJECT

Almost all sinkers are made from lead which is about 11 times heavier than water and are used to take an offering to the bottom or at least below the surface. The rule here is to use the least amount of weight necessary to accomplish the task. Too much weight is not only a poor decision, but it could cost you strikes. Keep in mind that the finer the diameter line you are using, the lighter the weight necessary to take the rig to the bottom. An angler fishing 10-pound test requires a smaller sinker than his partner using 15-pound test or 20-pound test when they are standing side by side.

Sinkers are made in hundreds of shapes tailored to handle specific jobs. You'll find plenty of local preferences, but a handful of the basic shapes will fill in nicely no matter

where you fish. The bank sinker is probably the most universal of all the designs. It manages to escape fouling pretty well on most bottoms and has reasonable holding power on a smooth bottom. Pyramid sinkers are a favorite of the surf fisherman because they tend to dig in and resist the pull of strong currents. Triangle and grapnel types anchor a bait in these situations.

The dipsy style does a nice job of rolling around the bottom and in those situations where you lift and lower an offering. Egg sinkers are a primary choice in tropical areas and small egg sinkers can be crimped on a leader to keep a trolling lure from sliding.

There are a number of torpedo-shaped trolling sinkers that help to keep a rig below the surface and work well with a straight pull. Anyone who tows baits or lures should always have a few of these on board. On the West Coast, cannon ball shapes are often used when mooching for salmon. They are often rigged to break away once the fish is hooked.

No matter where you fish or the species you seek, you should have an assortment of split shots in various light

Rubber-core sinkers and split shots are must items in every tackle box. They can be attached to a line in seconds when needed and removed just as quickly.

weights plus some rubber core types that can be slipped on the line. These do wonders in chum slicks when you want to get a bait deeper and in countless other situations where it might be necessary to add a bit of weight.

The worm weight or bullet sinker of fresh water fame has a myriad of uses in the marine environment and it pays to carry a selection ranging from 1/8 ounce to 1/2 ounce or more. Use them as stops when rigging a daisy chain and rely on them when rigging soft plastic lures. A worm weight and plastic tail make a great artificial for a variety of gamefish and can even be trolled by slipping a skirt over this combination.

Select each sinker carefully in terms of its weight, design and what you expect it to do. It takes a different sinker to anchor a bait than you would want if you expected the offering to slide along the bottom. Above all, remember to use the lightest weight consistent with your tackle and the conditions. In this case, smaller and lighter is better.

...nall, fast, seaworthy boats have opened the vista of the ocean to legions of fishermen.

MAKING THE CHOICE

A potential boat buyer is faced with a challenging task. He must decide on a rig that he believes will best suit his needs, outfit it accordingly, and be prepared to live with his selection. Possessing a basic understanding of the desired boat and the type of fishing it will be used for, one should not encounter major problems. In fact, the process can be fun and enlightening, culminating in a job that truly reflects an owner's personality.

Whether an angler is ready to part with thousands of dollars on quality merchandise or simply field the bare basics that will carry him to the fish, there are several factors that should influence his decision. He must consider the types of fish he'll be pursuing most and to what degree his family will fish with him. Any loving support from his wife may fall short if he invests in a boat that's heavy on the fishing and meager on the amenities. He'll also need to consider the range of his trips and check into fuel capacities. Then, there's the choice between the wave-slicing capabilities of a deep V hull for a smooth ride in rough seas or the economy of a modified V bottom. It makes little sense for a predominantly blue water fisherman to field a modified V hull that is likely to pound when it's confronted with angry seas. Conversely, a deep V entry is considered overkill and can actually be detrimental for shallow water, inshore fishing. As elementary as making that choice seems, enough expensive mistakes have been made to warrant a mention.

Large boats (over 26 feet) usually progress from cuddy cabins where there's a limited amount of forward shelter to full blown salon models. The big boat fisherman is generally blessed with an abundance of cockpit space. There's often enough standing room for several anglers to cast or bottom fish and a center mounted chair that's reserved for heavy game. Gunwales are usually tall enough and padded for an angler's security and comfort, and one should find adequate sized fish boxes and a live well underneath the cockpit deck hatches. Any creature comforts usually please the family. It's the complimenting blend of serious fishing and coziness that makes a large boat an attractive proposition, particularly if the owner is fortunate enough to employ a captain and mate. However, it's the small boater who must utilize his space wisely if he's to form a happy bond with his machine.

Cabin or cuddy models serve several useful purposes. They provide shade, comfort, and an abundance of dry storage. They effectively provide a buffer from the cold and less than kind seas, as well as comfortable overnight accommodations. Depending on the craft's size, most models will have adequate cockpit space for sincere fishing efforts. Several designs even have broad walk paths to the bow.

Center consoles or open fishermen are dedicated solely to those who desire the maximum fishing output from their vessels. The main concept behind this breed of boat is to provide 360 degrees of relatively unobstructed fishing room. Whereas cabin or cuddy models can be space restrictive, an angler can utilize every inch of a center console to his advantage. He can not only cast off the bow, but use it as a fighting platform to chase down a large fish. This technique is prominent on the offshore waters of the northeastern U.S. where anglers in small boats pursue large tuna. Should such an adversary take a trolling lure or a drifting bait, the unobstructive nature of the center console's design allows for a quick angler transfer to the bow. The captain then has the advantage of speed and accurate maneuverability as he chases down the fish to shorten the playing field. Excluding inboards and outboards that are bracketed onto a full transom, most center consoles aren't conducive to backing down on fish.

THE POWER CHOICE

Most of today's small boats are powered by outboards. The evolution of this engine over the years has made it extremely dependable, packing more horsepower per cubic inch, weighing less, and providing exceptional fuel efficiency (especially the loop charged designs). Because of their power and speed, they've enabled the small boater to fish waters that were once the exclusive domain of large sportfishing boats. These fishing distances often range from 40 to over 100 miles one way or a crossing from Florida to the Bahamas that can scale upwards of 130 miles to some of the resorts. Small boat anglers who plan on running considerable distances to find fish should seriously consider twin installations. The expense and fuel consumption of a second engine is a trade off for the security in knowing that you'll have the power to return to port should you encounter mechanical problems many miles off shore. A boat can plane and run on one engine, providing it isn't underpowered and that the outboards, mounted at the proper transom height, are equipped with properly pitched props. Before embarking on any offshore journey, an angler should be skilled and hold a strong respect for the sea. Anyone venturing forth without checking weather and filing a float plan only invites trouble and serious consequences.

A straight inboard or inboard/outboard powered boat prove the most fuel efficient. On a horsepower for horsepower basis, these power sources lack the torque and top end speed of an outboard, but offer the choice of burning regular or diesel fuel. If you have an interest in such power, consult your dealer first to find out if the package is available on a particular model. On an I/O model, you will then want to check and see the above deck engine hatch will drastically reduce cockpit fishing space. The midship positioning of a straight inboard apt to leave additional space in the cockpit. Also, raised engine hatches are sometimes used as a base for mounting the captain and passenger seats. Inboard power is available primarily on boats from 23 feet on up. However, there are a few companies that offer inboard versions in sizes between 17 and 22 feet. Whatever power option is selected, it's imperative to perform proper maintenance at designated intervals and burn only quality fuel and oil. If you do, you'll receive years of pleasurable performance in return.

FISH BOXES AND LIVE WELLS

When searching for the perfect boat, there will be several features you'll need to investigate. Again, think in terms of the fish you'll be pursuing. If weakfish, bluefish, blackfish or other small to medium size fish are the goals, you should find little problem with the size and capacity of most fish boxes. Tuna, dolphin, wahoo, and other large pelagics will require deep compartments measuring at least four feet in length. Check all holds for length and depth. A surprising number of mid-size boats are very weak in this department, requiring large ins ated coolers to ride along to handle the catch.

Factory fish boxes are often well-insulated, retaining cool temperatures to keep ice from melting. Some models will drain directly into the bilge, while others offer a direct channel overboard. On models where the drain is at or below water level, a plug will be necessary to prevent seawater seepage. Conversely, you'll need a means of discharging any melted ice and slush. One method is through a "duck bill" fitting which mounts over the transom drain holes. Water will be blocked out while drifting or slow trolling and drained from the box once the vessel reaches planing speed. A second option involves interrupting the drain line with a tee fitting. By running

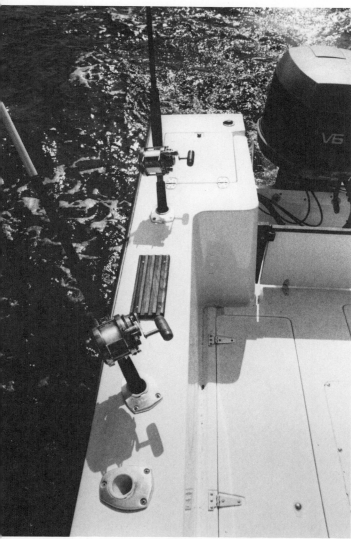

ach gunwale should have two or three flush-mounted rod olders. In this case, the aft holder points straight astern, the iddle one is angled at 45°, and the forward one at 90° for a ite rod or for use when drifting.

separate channel overboard and using a small electric pump, discharge can be extracted automatically with a flip of a vitch. You might consider a small screen over the inside fish ox drain to prevent any matter from clogging its passage.

Aside from icing fish, in-deck boxes should also be itable for dry storage including tackle boxes, life jackets,

etc. With a little modification, even gaffs can be fastened on the underside of a deck hatch, providing its surface is long and wide enough. They'll be out of the way here, yet readily accessible. Some captains secure a series of gaffs inside their cabin and on the forward bulkhead of center consoles. But beware, gaffs mounted in the open should be capped by a piece of surgical tubing to prevent a serious contact injury.

Almost all fishermen will experiment with live bait. Fortunately, built-in live wells are standard on most boats. A hold with a round or circular configuration will provide an unobstructed water flow. It will also keep bait, especially fin fish, healthy and lively longer by enabling them to freely swim against the current. If a large, portable well is not required, the only modification on a stock hold will be the addition of an aeration system. A healthy supply of bait depends on a rapid turnover of water. An adequate circulation system requires a main intake pump to supply fresh water and a high water pipe to discharge the excess once it reaches a specific level.

ROD STORAGE

Extra storage for both fishing rods and small items can be increased by a rocket launcher/leaning post combination. In addition, some models offer an integral tackle locker. Combine that with the space underneath, perfect for a cooler loaded with rigged baits or soft drinks, and you'll have a very versatile station.

Standard rod storage on most mid-size boats can be found under the gunwales. Depending upon the size of the boat, they can rack anywhere from two rods per side on up to six. They should be able to handle rods up to seven feet in length. The innovative fisherman always searches for extra storage and oftentimes has to create his own. Cabin models usually have sufficient forward overhead space that can handle a multitude of rods. Holders can be fastened to the ceiling or on the outside cuddy of walk around models. Holders can even be placed behind the captain and passenger stations.

Creating extra rod storage on an open boat is less challenging, providing you use the center console to its fullest extent. By measuring the length of a console's side and calculating the width of your larger reels, you'll be amazed by the job a custom receiver rack will do. It doesn't take long at

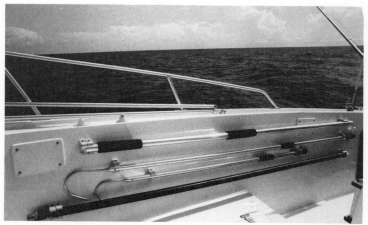

Gaffs should be located where they are out of the way, but easy to reach. Hook points should be turned inward or protected with plastic tubing to lessen the risk of injury.

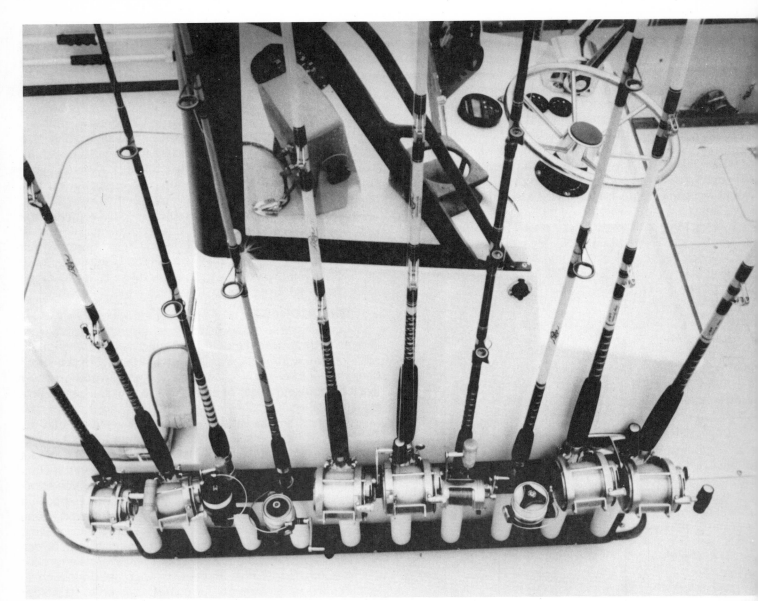

There is never enough rod stowage aboard a boat. Vertical rod holders along the console keep extra outfits ready and hand...

the local boat ramp or marina on a busy weekend to notice some of the more devoted center console fanatics. They'll often carry nearly ten rods on each side of the console.

A main advantage of vertical holders is that the rods are always handy. Various categories of tackle can be grabbed in a jiffy to cast to a passing fish, eliminating the valuable time it takes to free one from an under-the-gunwale holder. The vertical racks also store rods quickly and easily when clearing the deck to fight a fish. After the battle, the gear can be sorted out and deployed within seconds. When mounting this type of a holder, make sure to through bolt it to the console or bulkhead. They should be strong enough to support several heavy duty trolling outfits as well as a few spinning or bait casting rods.

Flush mounted, gunwale holders are often standard equipment. Some boat manufacturers provide a set of four receivers, but most will give you only two. In any event, trollers should seek four holders for maximum rod deployment,

concentrating on their positioning before they're installe... The slots designated for flat lines should angle directly off t... stern, while those to be used with the outriggers should ang... about 45 degrees outboard. By angling and possibly offsettin... the latter pair, there is less chance of the fishing lines draggin... across a flat line. Investing in additional rod holders w... enable you to increase a boat's fish-ability. Placing a pair... vertical receivers in any flat surface up forward or securin... them to the bow rail is ideal for drift fishing. They can als... double as holders for a kite rod/fishing outfit combinatio... when live baiting.

Shallow water skiffs can incorporate the same bas... ideas to obtain extra rod storage. A rocket launcher minus t... leaning post secured to the forward casting deck will add... least four outfits in a strategic position. Ditto in the stern.

GETTING HIGH

Flats skiffs or other shallow draft boats should b...

designed to operate in minimum depths. Part of the success of stalking shallow water fish lies in how quietly an angler approaches the unsuspecting quarry. An elevated platform offers the advantage of seeing fish from considerable distances, permitting an angler to plot out his best approach well in advance. Poling platforms are ideal for such situations. Pedestal chairs similar to those used on fresh water bass boats will also offer some elevation in addition to extra seating and comfortable casting.

The trolling motor's successful conversion from a fresh water to marine environment has enabled its manufacturers to cash in on this market. Owners of lightweight skiffs successfully use a pair of electric trolling motors to sneak up on fish or to simply wind down and cast in narrow, shallow creeks. The positioning of a trolling motor should correspond with the angler's habits. That is, it should be stern mounted if the angler plans on spending most of his time aft or secured forward if he plans on using the casting deck.

Other items worthy of consideration include sunshades and towers. Fish-spotting capabilities of the latter are obvious. However, on center consoles, you may want to select one that mounts directly to the deck instead of the gunwales to preserve walk around room. A major disadvantage of a tower on a small boat is that it can interfere with casting and, more importantly, also affect the craft's balance when someone is on top.

With a little planning, sunshades on center consoles can be incorporated into a functional unit. VHF antennae which operate on a line of sight basis and a loran C antenna can be advantageously mounted on top, along with a pair of small, lightweight outriggers. On the underside, an optional radio box will not only free up console space by accommodating electronics, but will protect them from the elements and theft if it has a good lock. One word of caution. Should you choose vertical rod holders with a sunshade, it's likely that your rods will interfere with the top. Tailored holes in the canvas above each rod holder can give you the best of both worlds.

OUTRIGGERS

Originally designed to space several trolling baits and to allow a drop back to fish such as sailfish or marlin, outriggers are considered routine on offshore boats. The size of the boat will dictate the size of the riggers, with boats up to 21 feet benefitting by the lighter poles which are approximately one inch in diameter at the base. Poles of 18 feet and nearing 2 1/2 inches in diameter are better suited for 22 to 26 foot boats. Larger boats carrying a wider beam will use longer riggers to spread their baits more effectively.

The action of a bait dangling from an outrigger will be influenced by the system's rigidity. Rigged natural baits such as mullet and ballyhoo and small artificials tend to have more appeal in conjunction with softer poles. A certain amount of whip governed by a compatible throttle speed will induce an attractive swimming/skipping action. Lighter outriggers are ideal for pursuing inshore species such as bluefish and mackerel and a host of offshore varieties including sailfish.

Marlin and tuna enthusiasts who routinely tow large natural baits such as mackerel, squid, and mullet, or medium large artificials, rely on the strength of heavy duty poles. The riggers must be stiff enough to "control" the large baits at high speeds, absorb tight outrigger clip settings, and counter vicious strikes from large fish. Spreaders add extra support and an aesthetic flare to the craft, but are usually considered overkill on small boats.

Outriggers should be mounted where they're convenient to the angler, ideally even with the console. Here they can be observed by the helmsman and are far enough forward so they won't interfere with the fishing line should the skipper have to chase down a fish bow first while the angler is still in the stern. If mounted properly, the outriggers will stand up to rigorous punishment in rough seas. It's always wise to through-bolt the outrigger bases to the gunwales. Never use screws, which tend to loosen and pull out. If the gunwales slope toward the bow or are tilted to one side, adding shim blocks should keep the mounts level. Back-up blocks should be used under the gunwales to reinforce the mounting surface, reducing stress damage to the gelcoat and fiberglass.

Monofilament line of around 300 pound test and nylon cord are the most common choices when stringing an outrigger. A drawback with mono is that it stretches and will eventually reduce the amount of tension on the pole. Nylon cord stretches also, but it springs back to its original length and may last longer. Most brands of outrigger clips utilize a pin or wire that is compressed between two caps, forming a fishing line restraint. An audible sound is usually heard when it is tripped. Clips should be checked for their maximum adjustable tension. It doesn't make sense to install clips that can't secure a heavy bait in choppy seas. There are a couple of manufacturers marketing clips with ball bearing rollers which allow fishing lines to actually roll with every tug of the line, reducing abrasive wear. A major advantage of this clip is that its tension can be precisely adjusted to lock in large lures. But beware. Oversetting these clips can buckle an outrigger, if a fish fails to pull the heavy monofilament free. In addition, a pair of clips mounted to a boat's transom eyes can increase the effectiveness of the flat lines by reducing the angle at which they enter the water. They are great when it comes to keeping the lures or baits that are riding just off the transom in the water under rough sea conditions.

As a final, yet effective touch, a 4/0 or similar size reel can be mounted on the base of a rigger pole to string a teaser. The teaser line, usually 100 pound test monofilament, is run through the rigger's first guide, through the center of a cork ball so the line can't slide back through the guide, and then tied to a snap swivel. A favorite teaser is then attached and dropped back so that it rides just outside of any prop wash. An inexpensive alternative to the teaser reel is to fasten two bolts about six inches apart and a couple of feet up one of the rigger poles. The teaser line can then be tied to one of the bolts and, when not in use, it can be wrapped around the two bolts. A teaser can also be tied off to a cleat. Just remember to pull them in before backing down on a fish.

FIGHTING CHAIRS

Another offshore option worthy of consideration is a fighting chair. With the current popularity of stand up gear combined with the fact that the majority of small boat fishermen use gear no heavier than 50 pound test, a full size chair isn't vital. The standard factory-installed chair or a small retrofitted model will do just fine, providing the positioning of the chair has been thought out carefully. By placing a person with a standard size trolling rod in the chair, you can check any clearance problems with the outboard(s). It's also advantageous to center the chair so that the angler's feet can rest on the transom door or gunwales. A gimbal is necessary to accommodate the rod butt.

An increasing number of boats, even walk-around cuddy models, are appearing with foredeck mounted chairs. To receive the optimum advantage, follow the same guidelines for mounting a chair on the stern, making sure the angler can reach the gunwales with his feet. If there's a bow rail, don't let it interfere with the fishing line. With some precise planning, the rail can be incorporated into a rod rest. An under-the-deck back-up plate, often a quarter or half inch aluminum, is mandatory when bolting in a fighting chair. The lever action of the chair along with the stress of an angler pushing off the gunwale with his feet may exert an incredible amount of pressure on the deck. Bolts mounted directly into wood or fiberglass tend to pull free under such pressure. Backing plates also are recommended on all deck mounted chairs for safety reasons.

ELECTRONICS

Mounting electronics on small boats is relatively easy, if you use the console advantageously. Flats skiffs and shallow water boats intended for sound and estuary fishing can maximize valuable console space by utilizing in-dash displays such as water temperature or digital depth readings. If some form of depth indicator is desired, the compact size of a liquid crystal display recorder may be an attractive buy. Make certain the unit will permit proper throttle clearance if it is to be positioned on top of the console. A VHF and possibly a conventional graph recorder can also be included by modifying some of the storage space underneath the console.

The designs and sizes of some of the mid-range boats can easily accommodate a loran and chart recorder as well as an assortment of in dash gauges. The trick is to lay the electronics out in a highly visible fashion that's convenient to the angler. You can eliminate problems by having covers made for all electronics that are exposed to the elements and taking the time to spray the connections with a lubricant after each trip.

SAFETY AT SEA

No matter how much fish-ability has been incorporated into a boat, no one should set forth without an array of essential safety gear. Safety at sea should be more of a concern than actually catching fish, yet it is often one of the most overlooked aspects of boating. Aside from carrying the required U.S.C.G. equipment (flares, fog horn, life jackets, throw cushions and fire extinguisher), the conscientious boater should invest in other products that he may have to depend on in an emergency situation.

Imperative safety equipment that is worthy of investigation includes an EPIRB (Emergency Position Indicating Radio Beacon), strobe lights, portable VHF, and a life raft. Fortunately, there's an increasing acceptance of life rafts aboard small recreational boats, mainly because of the recent advan-

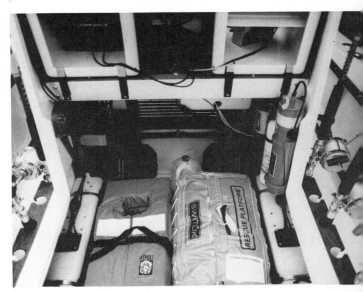

Safety at sea should be paramount. In addition to plenty life jackets, this center-console carries a life raft and an EPIR unit that will activate automatically in an emergency.

cements in their design and compact sizes. The advantages a life raft are obvious. They are much easier to spot during search and rescue mission. They significantly reduce t chance of death from drowning, hypothermia, and sha attack, and they present the opportunity to keep everyo together until help arrives. There are some models geared the small boater that sell for less than a thousand dollars a are compact enough to fit inside a console or in a cuddy.

Life jackets or Personal Flotation Devices (PFD) are oth safety items that are often misunderstood. There are four typ of recreational PFDs, each one meriting review before p chase. Not unlike the boat and its accessories, the selection life jackets should be coordinated with your type of fishing. F example, if your fishing is limited to heavily populated bays sounds, increasing the odds of an early rescue, a type design can be of service. A type III rating is a vest-like jacl that's comfortable to wear. It's designed so that the wearer c be placed in a vertical and slightly backward position, witho a tendency to turn him face down. A type II jacket is similar t type III, in that it's designed to turn the wearer to a vertical a slightly backward position and is sized for ease of emerger donning. It's also recommended on the same waters as a ty III. A type I PFD has the greatest buoyancy and will turn m unconscious persons in the water from a face down positi to a vertical and slightly backward position. This type recommended for waters where there will likely be a delay rescue. Type IV constitutes the throw cushions, which a designed to be grasped and held by the user in a m overboard situation. At least one throw cushion per boa should be purchased. All safety equipment, i.e. life rafts, PF flares, EPIRB, and drinking water, should be stored togethe an area where they can be offloaded in seconds.

Strategy, efficiency, and thoughtful planning are all ess tial when purchasing and rigging a new boat. By keeping saf a major consideration and setting up the craft to suit your o needs, you're bound to derive years of enjoyment. There boat that'll suit everyone's needs.

USING ELECTRONICS

LORAN (LOng RAnge Navigation) is an electronic system using shore-based radio transmitters and shipboard receivers to enable boaters and fishermen to determine their positions at sea. The receiver measures the Time Differences (TD) between pulses of a master and two secondary stations ashore. Before the introduction of loran C and the competitive prices that put such units within reach of the average boater, locating productive fishing spots and traveling to remote regions depended highly on the captain's ability to decipher navigational formulas or to incorporate visual reference points.

When it wasn't possible to line up land ranges, experienced captains searching for structure used to calculate the time it took their boats to cover a known distance at a specific r.p.m., paying particular attention to sea conditions. Once they concluded the timed, trial run on that particular day, they would track the bearings of the wreck or drop-off and estimate their time of arrival.

A captain was forced to keep his speed constant throughout the entire run. At the plotted location, a marker jug was deployed and the chart recorder monitored closely for signs of the target. Executing this formula was challenging, to say the least. Should the seas kick-up while underway forcing a reduction in speed, it was often back to the stopwatch and calculator to salvage the day.

The loran C unit greatly simplified navigational duties and maximized actual fishing time. The system is a pulsed, low frequency (100 KHz), hyperbolic, radio-navigational system utilizing a chain of three to five shore based transmitting stations. A Master and at least two Secondary transmitting stations comprise each chain, which releases an association of pulses at specified Group Repetition Intervals (GRI). The loran C chain for a designated area is determined electronically by the individualized GRI, with some nine series applying to U.S. regions.

The Master station transmitter identifies and synchro-

oran C enables a fisherman to return repeatedly to a productive structure.

nizes the loran C chain. Pulsed signals transmitted by two Secondary stations are synchronously timed with the Master station. The synchronized pulses are then transmitted at precise time intervals and processed by the loran C unit to measure the distance in the time required for these pulses to reach the shipboard receiver from each of the transmitters. The difference in time is sensibly referred to as Time Difference (TD). The TDs appear on a digital readout display and give the boater his current position.

The various types of loran on the market today all have their own form of operations. However, the first procedure with any new loran is to dial in the applicable chain, followed by selecting the secondaries best suited for the area. With some units, it's only necessary to program the chain initially, providing you stay within the specified region. After the four digit chain is entered, the best available secondaries should be selected. Each master-secondary pair produces one Line of Position (LOP). For accuracy, you'll want to choose secondaries that provide you with LOP crossing angles that are close to 90 degrees, which can be determined on a loran C overprinted navigational chart. After locking in the desired secondaries, the unit will display in microseconds the vessel's location (Lines of Position or LOP). With the aid of a loran C chart, a captain can visualize the exact position of his vessel by locating the point where the two LOPs intersect.

Programming a unit involves entering specified waypoints. For example, once an angler has the coordinates to a deep water wreck and the basic start-up procedures have been followed, he'll enter the twelve digits of the site and wait several seconds for his unit to display the pertinent tracking information, such as the course to steer and the distance to the waypoint. From there, it's just a matter of tracking down the coordinates to his destination. He'll also have the option of recalling his point of departure coordinates from the unit's memory for an equally efficient ride home. Loran C units vary in price and capabilities, with the more advanced designs featuring both Latitude/Longitude and TDs, time to waypoint, arrival, anchor watch and off course alarms, vessel speed, tracking mode, vast memory storage, etc..

The role loran C plays in fishing is immeasurable. It allows the bottom fisherman to record productive or new spots he has discovered, building a circuit of numbers. Seasoned anglers have thick books with loran numbers, marking the slightest breaks in the ocean floor that have yielded a good catch to wrecks measuring over 100 feet in length. Depending upon the season and the predominant species, these perceptive fishermen usually run down a series of numbers during the course of a day. Unless one area is teeming with life, the usual routine consists of working each site for about 15 minutes before moving to the next locale.

Breaks in the reefline, major underwater humps, or deep drop-offs are areas where baitfish and gamefish lurk. By gaining access to these points, or by discovering some on your own, you can maximize productive fishing time. Even the blue water angler who plies the ocean's surface for signs of fish can use the loran C to his advantage. Hard bottom or structure will remain constant, but wind and currents continually alter the positions of rips, eddies, weedlines, and water temperature variations. These features can often be relocated the following

The graph depth sounder with its detailed print out ranks a the primary unit for the angler who wants maximum identi fication of underwater structure. Modern machines boast countless array of features operated by a push button ke pad.

day with a respectable degree of accuracy, providing the coordinates were recorded.

The same holds true for schooling fish. Should excep tional fishing occur within a certain region and the lora numbers are placed into memory, an angler can minimize h searching to find them the next day. Even highly migratory fis will remain in areas for considerable periods of time, provic

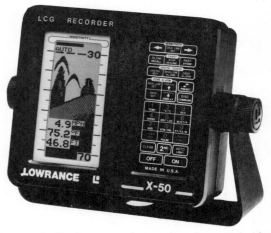

Liquid crystal displays are becoming increasingly popul among depth sounder users. In addition to displaying graph, this unit provides digital depth readout, water ter perature, and boat speed.

ing there's an abundance of baitfish to satisfy their hunger. Th incorporating angler will often take the procedure one ste further by factoring in current speed and wind directic before attempting to relocate the fish.

Aside from increasing a fisherman's potential, a loran C a highly accurate navigational aid. Taking and storing an inle LOP on the way offshore will virtually guarantee an efficie and exacting ride back home. In the past, captains had compensate for a current's speed and sea conditions in plc ting a course. Loran C units have simplified the procedure computing all of the variables internally. Returning to home port is simply a matter of entering the respective coordinates and tracking them back down, after allowing the machine several seconds to acquire and compute the input. The unit will continually compensate for variations in boat speed, currents, seas, etc., guiding the captain on the straightest course to his destination. The obvious advantages will be the savings in time and fuel, particularly offshore of the Gulf Coast and northeastern states where it's common to run between 60 and 100 miles in search of fish.

Safety at sea is increased with a loran. A smart captain keeps the coordinates of his home port plus other havens within striking distance of it close at hand. He'll have piece of mind knowing that one of the various inlets may offer an "escape route" if threatening weather moves between him and his home destination. He'll be able to decide on his clearest and most feasible path by entering several choices into the loran and comparing the mileage and heading to each site. Small boat anglers who fish many miles offshore of the South Florida coast during the summer are aware of the severe thunderstorms that frequently move seaward. The knowledgeable captain will monitor such weather and will not hesitate to use his loran to plot an alternate route home if he is threatened. Furthermore, should the boater find himself in an emergency situation many miles from land, reading his current LOP to the Coast Guard or another boater will greatly facilitate his rescue.

Learning the basic operations of a loran C receiver is not a difficult task. It may seem somewhat complicated at first, but a thorough explanation by a knowledgeable electronics salesman combined with a few practice sessions will make it easy. The more familiar you become with a unit, the more you'll investigate its other features. Before long, you'll wonder how you ever fished without it. It should be noted that the loran C is merely an aid in navigation and should never be depended upon exclusively. There is still no substitute for a vast knowledge of seamanship and every journey should include a close watch of the compass and various other landmarks, depth ranges, buoys, etc. Also, invest in a quality loran C chart, taking the time to familiarize yourself with the boat's current LOP.

RECORDERS

It wasn't long ago when anglers were faced with a relatively limited choice of fish finders. If you owned a large craft and had the available console space, you were among the fortunate few who could accommodate a quality product. The size and bulkiness of most of these units left a lot to be desired. They were still effective in monitoring structure and revealing fish, and had the depth range to satisfy most deep water interests. The small boater, however, was somewhat limited in his choice and had to settle for smaller units that were usually lacking in performance.

Enter the computer age. Today's lineup of electronics is so diversified that it actually creates a great deal of confusion for first time buyers. There are color videos, graph recorders, liquid crystal displays, flashers, and digital sonars, most of which feature state of the art components. Selecting a unit that best performs to the consumer's fishing needs will provide him with years of prosperous outings.

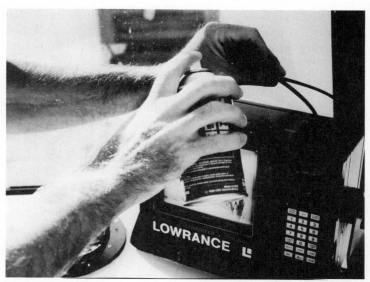

Electronics aboard a boat require periodic maintenance. Contacts and connections corrode, causing poor or lost signals. Spray them frequently with an anti-corrosive.

Among the most sophisticated units are the color videos featuring a CRT (cathode ray tube) display. Their ability to distinguish targets from the bottom in various colors (including concentrations of fish as well as individual members) plus an expansive depth range have made them a viable investment among commercial fishermen. The strongest echoes, which represent fish at close range, will usually appear dark, with the weaker signals consisting of lighter hues. While the size of some CRT videos have been reduced, most are still too large for the average small boat. Bear in mind that CRT displays are susceptible to direct sunlight, requiring a reasonable amount of shade for maximum viewing potential. Their costs also keep them out of the budgets of many small boaters.

The paper or graph recorder is the most popular sonar device on the market. The unit's ability to acutely depict the ocean floor has endeared it to anglers with a sincere interest in locating bottom fish. Structure often comprises an ecosystem that supports numerous marine species, and a successful day often hinges on finding such locations. A quality graph recorder has the ability to distinguish between hard bottoms that are likely to attract fish, and soft or muddy bottoms. This is determined by the grayline displayed below the actual bottom line, with a wide band generally representing hard bottom and a narrow band mostly characteristic of soft terrain.

Properly fine tuning a unit by coordinating the sensitivity or gain (the degree of amplification of a sonar signal needed to create an image) with a minimal amount of suppression (a feature which discriminates against both mechanical and electrical noise) will create a precise bottom definition revealing prominent structure. Any bait or gamefish that may be within the cone sphere of the ultrasonic beam emitting from the transducer will also be shown. Some of the more advanced designs even offer programmable upper and lower limits, expanding the bottom picture in increments as little as one foot. Even the smallest baitfish or bottom features stand out.

Let's assume you're deep jigging for grouper and snapper

over a reef in 180 feet of water. While the graph in its normal operating range will clearly define the bottom and fish (appearing as small boomerangs), the intensity of the picture can be increased by reducing the upper limit to 130 feet and setting the bottom limit at 200 feet. This so called zone or window will focus on that 70 foot segment where the fish are likely to be, resulting in a more defined reproduction of the ocean floor. Another feature of certain graph recorders is their ability to interface with a loran. The productive coordinates stored in a loran's memory will print instantly on the graph paper by simply pressing a button. When reviewing the roll of paper, an angler will have the numbers as well as a prominent description of any structure, wreck, depression, or rockpile encountered during the trip. He will then be able to log the coordinates and an illustration of the find into his loran book.

A device often used in conjunction with a graph recorder is a digital sonar. This instrument is more of a navigational aid than a fish finder, since its primary purpose is to inform a boater of the depth. It can offer an advance warning to a captain who is running into shallow water and also aid in determining the whereabouts of land by monitoring the depths, should a loran go on the blink many miles offshore. Some of the better units include shallow and deep alarms that can double as effective anchor watches.

Such a unit can benefit the offshore troller, primarily by checking his depth and keeping him within certain boundaries

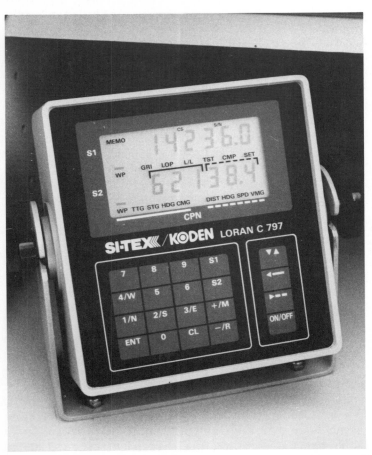

Compact, Loran C units fit on consoles and enable small boat fishermen to find precise spots repeatedly. They also give you a direct course home when the day is over.

or in the vicinity of a deep drop-off. Digitals are perfect for staying on top of such structures and can be left on all day without the inconvenience of replacing chart paper. They're also successfully used by inshore anglers who want to keep tabs on channel edges, as well as bay and sound depths. These units come in diameters of less than three inches for in-dash applications and slightly larger bracket-mounted models for console top displays.

Flashers constitute an inexpensive way to check water depths. Like the digitals, they can be fixed in-dash or mounted on a bracket and, similar to graph recorders, can reveal a bottom's composition by the width of their signal. Flashers rely on a brush system that makes contact on the scan disk's collector rings, with most of their depth ranges inshore of 300 feet. Because of the limited depth, they appeal mostly to the bay or sound fisherman. Unlike graph units, flashers are a bit more complicated to read. After they lock in, any obstruction between the bottom and surface will appear as a signal regardless of whether it's a fish or structure. Fishermen who are familiar with their terrain and these units can usually decipher such readings.

The current wave of advanced technology in the sonar industry brought the Liquid Crystal Display (LCD) unit into play. Similar to a graph recorder, an LCD unit depicts the bottom on a screen and offers many advanced features. It operates without paper, relying on pixels (tiny squares) that light up on the screen to illustrate a water column. Their ultra compact sizes can challenge the digitals for those who prefer constant depth readings without sacrificing paper. A troller relying on a digital readout can keep within a specified bottom contour, but an LCD unit will show the bottom visually plus any fish. By locating a concentration of bait, a captain can swing the boat around and work the area thoroughly, even lowering an offering on a downrigger.

Current LCD sonars are so sophisticated that they can automatically set and adjust their own upper and lower ranges or be programmed manually. They come with alarm zones, speedometers, water temperature and digital depth displays, zoom features, and mileage log. Some even offer menus with simple instructions on how to operate the various features.

Before selecting a recorder, the fisherman must take into account the type of fish he pursues most. An angler who enjoys chasing bluefish along the northeast coast might be satisfied with an LCD, but the hard core bottom fisherman may be better off with the precise details offered by a graph recorder. Whatever the selection, it's imperative that the unit and transducer be installed by a knowledgeable person. And remember, keep transducer and power cables away from engine and bilge pump wiring and VHF antennae to limit the potential for electrical interference.

Transducer selection will also depend on your fishing. If your game is bottom fishing in waters shallower than 300 feet, a transducer with a high operating frequency (192 – 200 kHz) will provide excellent depth penetration. You'll also want to investigate transducer cone angles. If most of your fishing is done inside of 100 feet of water, you'll get a better definition of fish and see more of the area around you with a medium cone angle (about 20 degrees), whereas going with a narrow cone angle (approximately 8 degrees) will concentrate the sound nergy and lend a sharper picture in greater depths. A wide one angle (45 degrees) and a 50 kHz transducer may be the est combination for a downrigger fishermen and those who re interested in viewing a greater portion of the surrounding reas.

A transducer operating on a low frequency (50 kHz) with 30 degree cone angle will provide greater depth penetration deep waters. Offshore fishermen who continually fish over anyons, walls, and other deep edges in depths as great as 500 feet rely on such a combination to locate concentrations f squid and other bait that can lead to gamefish. Although a ow frequency transducer and a quality graph recorder gener- lly result in good vertical resolution, the definition of under- ater objects (including fish) will not be quite as sharp in hallow water as those of a high frequency transducer. Sonar eared for deep water explorations will experience a reduc- on in quality in waters shallower than 100 feet. Again, discuss ur needs with an authorized dealer to determine the proper ansducer combination.

A surface temperature gauge is another imperative item. eteran anglers from the shallows to the deep know that ertain fish react differently to variations in water temperature. outh Florida guides, for example, know that tarpon prefer ater temperatures right around 75 degrees, and readings wer than that can delay their migration into the region.

An angler can use such a gauge to predict the arrival of ansient fish or to search out sections of productive water. una fishermen who ply their trade over the canyons of the ortheast realize that a sudden jump in water temperature ithin a relatively short span can indicate the presence of a arm water eddy or gyre (circulating portions of a warm water urrent that break away from the main flow). Such a presence r pocket of warm water often carries impressive numbers of oth bait and gamefish. A digital temperature gauge can be ounted in dash or on a bracket and some are contained ithin graph and LCD units. All vital electronics should be rned on at the dock and checked routinely.

MARINE RADIO

Of all the electronics available to a boater, none is as portant as a VHF radio. Communication at sea is essential hen trying to get a handle on the fishing action and, most portantly, in guaranteeing your safety.

A VHF is a high frequency radio operating on a "line of ght" principal. That is, communication is optimum when the ntenna of a base station or ship has a clear path to transmit to e one on your vessel. In contrast to the more expensive ngle side band unit (SSB) which operates on a low frequency d has an average range of 500 miles, a VHF aboard a boat ell offshore is likely to have difficulty reaching a base station land. When planning an offshore run, anglers should tempt to establish contact with another captain or two eaded in the same direction. By keeping lines of communica- on open, you'll be more assured of a safe outing.

VHF radios are susceptible to the elements. It's impera- e to mount them in areas offering the best protection. owever, keep a VHF away from the compass, where their agnets will result in erroneous readings. Small boaters can d space within console compartments if their boat doesn't

Sophisticated electronics have revolutionized fishing. This skipper monitors a depth sounder as he follows a compass course.

already have a designated radio box, or they can be mounted on a bracket inside a console access hatch. If the unit has to be mounted on the console's dash, invest in a protective weather cover. However, make certain to acquire material such as acrylon that can breathe and eliminate condensation. Even a minimum amount of moisture will be detrimental. Also, remember that by mounting an antenna on a T-top or tower you'll enjoy greater signal penetration.

Aside from boat to boat communications, VHFs provide access to land based marine operators who can direct dial both local and long distance telephone numbers for you. And, as a safety feature, the U.S. Coast Guard continually monitors channel 16. Whereas the inland or beach fisherman will suffice with one VHF, the respecting offshore boater often opts for peace of mind and carries two radios, complete with separate antennae. Even a back-up, hand-held radio is a sound idea. After all, safety at sea should be a primary concern.

HOW TO SHARPEN A HOOK

SIDE CUT

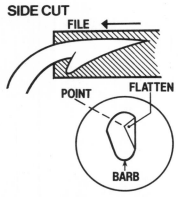

Used on new hooks out of the box, the SIDE CUT flattens one side, reducing wire diameter. With the point of the hook on top and the eye toward you, lay the sharpening tool against one side of the hook, keeping it parallel. Make several strokes toward the bend of the hook until that side is flattened. Don't flatten both sides.

DIAMOND

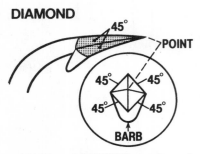

A properly formed DIAMOND produces four cutting edges plus a sharp point that many anglers consider the ultimate. It is nothing more than two Half-Diamonds back to back with one on top of the hook point and the second against the barb.

HALF DIAMOND

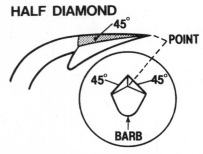

The HALF-DIAMOND ranks as the most popular method for sharpening hooks because it is effective and easy. Make a Standard Cut on one side of the point (opposite the barb) and a second Standard Cut on the other side. Done correctly, it produces a cutting edge on top and minor ones on either side.

TRIANGLE

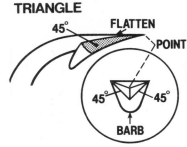

Triangulation develops three cutting edges, but it takes time to do. It's worth the effort where the rewards are important. Start by laying the sharpening tool at right angles to the top of the hook point. Hold the hook the same way you would in other methods. Flatten the top of the hook and then put a Half-Diamond Cut on the underside of the point against the barb, forming a TRIANGLE.

STANDARD CUT

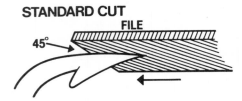

The STANDARD CUT is the basic stroke for most hook sharpening. With the point of the hook on top and the eye toward you, lay the tool against one side at a 45° angle. Stroking should be done from the point toward the bend. If you stroke from the bend toward the point, there may be a burr or nub on the point that must be removed.

SHORT BARB

Think of a barb as a wedge that hinders penetration. By reducing the height of the barb, it's easier to get a hook in a hard-mouthed fish. Both barbless and short barbed hooks hold surprisingly well and penetrate effectively.

SHORT POINT

Driving a hook point into the mouth of a fish may prove difficult on some species. Shortening the point and then resharpening it is one way to increase the odds with tarpon, billfish, and other animals with cinder block mouths.

SETTING THE HOOK

Setting the hook involves more than instinctively rearing back on the rod and hoping for the best. Preparation, timing, and technique play critical roles in reducing the number of missed opportunities. On some days, strikes are few and far between. You can't fight a fish until you bury the barb in its jaw. That's why the tales of the one that got away far outstrip those of trophies landed or intentionally released.

Fishing breaks down into two major areas. Once you find the quarry and get it to attack bait or lure, you pick up the gauntlet of hooking, fighting, and landing that critter. Both aspects are equally demanding and combine to form the total angling experience.

HOOKS

Choosing the right hook for the species you intend to catch and the tackle you have selected, becomes an essential element of success. The lighter the wire from which a hook is made, the easier it will penetrate a fish's mouth. Obviously, there are reasonable limitations that range from the strength of the jaws to the tackle. If you are using heavy gear, a fine wire hook will straighten the first time you play tug-of-war. With huskier gear, you need stouter hooks. Just the opposite applies to the light tackle enthusiast. Trying to drive an oversized hook home with thin line and a whippy rod borders on the impossible, particularly when the fish in question has a jaw made from reinforced concrete or cinder blocks. As a rule, opt for the smallest size and minimum strength consistent with the tackle.

A barbless hook penetrates more easily than one with a pronounced barb. The greater the angle on the barb and the longer its length, the more difficult it is to set. That barb becomes a wedge rather than a spear. For species with very hard mouths, it pays to file the barb, reducing the taper and shortening the length.

The majority of hooks being manufactured today lack the degree of sharpness necessary to insure an impressive percentage of hookups. New hooks taken directly from the box should be touched up with any of the dozens of tools on the market designed for that purpose. Every hook point on plugs or lures with two or three sets of trebles should be reworked before that artificial is fished. Sharpening not only makes a difference, but it is probably the primary factor responsible for a poor hookup ratio.

Sharpening correctly centers on creating a point that will hang on flesh the minute it touches and then have the taper to penetrate easily. Unless the point is sharp enough to hang, the hook has no chance of penetrating. You can test the point by drawing it over your thumbnail. If it slides, it doesn't have the necessary sharpness.

A hook with an exceedingly sharp point will penetrate the mouth of most fish if the wire from which the hook was made is light enough. On larger hooks and when faced with rough-mouthed adversaries, it pays to put cutting edges in the point of the hook. A diamond shape is the best with four cutting edges: top, bottom, right side, and left side. You can get by in many cases with edges on the top and sides. Triangulation where the bottom and two sides are flattened also does a nice job.

The importance of hook sharpening cannot be over-emphasized. It is vital and should be performed as routinely as tying strong knots. This simple preparation makes a difference. Regardless of the tool you use for sharpening at home, carry a file, stone, or battery-operated sharpener on the water for instant touchups.

STRIKING A FISH

No matter how or when you set the hook, the line between you and the fish must be tight and the tip of the rod must point directly at the fish before starting any upward or sideward movement. Everything after that becomes a matter of refinement of technique. Too many anglers instinctively rear back on the rod when they feel a tug at the other end or they see a fish engulf the offering. That merely alerts the fish that something is unnatural, usually resulting in the bait being dropped. With the exception of a few notorious, bottom-dwelling, bait stealers, you have much more time to set the hook than you suspect.

Getting the line tight depends on circumstances. If the fish starts to move off smartly, you simply throw the reel in gear

Holding a fish correctly when removing the hook reduces the chance of injury. Pressing firmly on the spots at the back of a jack's gill covers keeps the fish relatively immobile.

To test sharpness, drag a hook point over the thumbnail. Unless it hangs, it isn't sharp enough.

at the appropriate time, drop the rod tip, wait until you feel the line straining, and you're ready to set. It should be noted that some experts advocate maintaining this pressure against hard-mouthed fish such as tarpon without ever bringing the rod back to set. That came about because there is a tendency to set too soon and pull the hook.

If the fish is not moving off fast enough or if it stays in the same area, use the reel to recover line and get tight on your quarry. Drop the rod tip and point it at the fish, cranking as rapidly as you can. Whatever method you use, a sharp hook and a tight line tilt the odds in your favor.

Largemouth bass aficionados suggest that one plant the barb with a mighty yank tailored to turn the boat over and cross the eyes of the fish in the process. Scales don't have opinions. If you put one where the bass is supposed to be and followed this procedure, you would be amazed at how little force is transmitted to the hook. It's virtually impossible to drive a nail with a single blow from a hammer and the same holds true of setting a hook. With the line tight and the rod tip pointing at the fish, use a series of short, sharp jerks to bury the barb in the jaw of the critter on the other end.

There are several arguments for striking sideways with the rod low and parallel to the water. For one thing, you achieve a straighter pull rather than an upward force. That not only aids hooking, but it keeps the bait or lure in the area of the fish if you should miss. An upward yank will pull a topwater offering or trolled bait clear of the water and several yards from the fish. Side strikes hold the bait a foot or two in front of the target no matter how hard you tug. If you lock your arms and rotate the body, you can generate a lot more force with the side strike. It takes practice before you do this without having to think about it.

Knowing when to strike carries the same importance as how to strike. If a fish plans to engulf a natural bait or artificial, it must first blow the water in its mouth out through the gills. Some species that have crushers in the back of their throats generally toss everything back there first. With a live bait, give the fish time to swim off with it, turn the bait around in its mouth, and start to swallow it before you come tight and strike. Timing is critical. One clue occurs when the fish starts to move off steadily. If you are dropping back to a billfish, tarpon, or any species that jumps and the fish suddenly clears the surface while you are dropping back, your quarry already knows it has been duped and is trying to get rid of the bait. Put the tip down

and crank as fast as you can until the line comes tight. Then, s◆ the hook.

In a chum slick, it often pays to let the fish pick up th◆ offering and ease off before you set. Extend your arms and th◆ rod toward the fish. When the line is straining, you can reac◆ Learning to hook fish consistently takes experience. If you a◆ setting quickly and miss a fish or two, try delaying. If you a◆ giving the fish plenty of time and come up with a bare hoo◆ shorten the process.

The most dangerous situation in terms of missing the fi◆ takes place when you can see your quarry clearly. It opens i◆ mouth and inhales natural or artificial. You see it happen ar◆ instinctively jerk the rod. Cool courage dictates a bett◆ approach. Wait until the fish closes its mouth and turns awa◆ from you before working to get the line tight. It's a toug◆ exercise the first few times, but if you can master the tec◆ nique, the fish is yours.

With very light lines, you don't have the luxury of settir◆ with any degree of force. Thin wire hooks become an impo◆ tant adjunct with points sharpened to perfection. Frequent◆ the angler simply starts to reel when the fish has the bait or lu◆ relying on the hooks to bury themselves when tension ◆ maintained.

SETTING THE DRAG

The drag on the reel should be set before you sta◆ fishing. For the typical fishing situation using lines testing ◆ pounds or lighter, establish a drag setting of 15 percent of th◆ unknotted line strength. Use a scale to insure accuracy. Th◆ measurement is taken with the line attached to the hook ◆ the scale and the rod tip pointing directly at the scale. Wi◆ this approach, you'll need about 3 pounds of drag with ◆ pound test line, 2 pounds of drag with 15 pound test and ◆ forth. Remember that you take the measurement on a straig◆ pull. If a fish is swimming away rapidly and you point the r◆ tip directly at it, that will be the least amount of drag.

For lines over 20 pound test and up through 50 pound, ◆ percent of the breaking strength is adequate drag. You can ◆ to 30 percent drag for 80 pound and 130. With heavier tack◆ there is a tendency to measure drag through the rod as if◆ were in fighting position. It is still better to measure all drag ◆ a straight pull so that you know the minimum amount.

Once you lift the rod above the horizontal, the dr◆ begins to increase because of the curvature of the rod bla◆ and the friction against the guides. As the amount of line ◆ the spool decreases, the drag increases. All of these effec◆ are cumulative. That's why it is important to use a modera◆ initial setting and use your hands to increase the drag wh◆ necessary.

Some of the latest reels allow the angler to change dr◆ settings easily and a few even remember the previous settir◆ Adjusting the drag while fighting a fish is a dangerous practi◆ and one that should be reserved for experienced fisherme◆ With reasonable settings, you can add extra pressure wi◆ your hand on the reel and take it off just as quickly if the fi◆ surges.

There are special situations where the problem becom◆ one of stopping a fish from reaching the sanctuary of a wre◆ reef, or other structure. Possibly, your task is to snake th◆

critter out from under a dock or alongside a piling. Desperate measures are required and it then makes sense to increase the initial drag setting. If the fish reaches the haven, it's all over anyway, so you have to give it that old try.

Certain species such as bonefish put on spectacular dashes when hooked. They'll streak across a shallow flat like a hydroplane at full throttle. Cranking down on the drag risks line breakage and is counterproductive to the reason you hook a bonefish.

SLUGGING IT OUT

The instant a fish feels a hook's steel in its mouth, it will take off like a drag racer getting the green light. That creature wants to get out of there right now. For some species, this means a lengthy run; for others, it is a dive toward the bottom. Assuming your drag is set properly, there is nothing you can do but wait until the fish stops. If you clamp down and apply too much pressure, the line will pop like bakery string.

During this run, you're holding the rod at a 45 degree angle so that the fish fights the extra pressure. With a particularly large or fast fish making an excessive run, you may want to drop the rod tip and point it right at the fish. This reduces the amount of drag and produces the minimum resistance at the reel. Keep in mind that all the line being towed through the water tends to increase the drag, so you are beginning to compensate.

In extreme situations where the line left on the spool is dwindling rapidly, there is a natural tendency to tighten the drag adjustment to stop the run. That is a costly error. The correct procedure is to back off on the drag since it is increasing as the spool diameter decreases. You may have to follow the fish with the boat. If you do, resist the temptation to angle directly for the fish. Tests show that this puts incredible pressure on the line, causing it to break. Instead, follow the line through the water until you reach the fish.

A fishing rod is not a derrick and the reel is not a winch. To recover line, you must pump the fish toward you. This is done by lifting the rod smoothly and dropping the rod tip as you reel in the controlled slack. If done correctly, the line is tight all of the time. When you can move the fish easily, long, full pumps from the water to about a 75 degree angle make sense. On a fish that is deep or stubborn, try short pumps. You may only regain a half turn of line each time, but the technique can be very effective.

Handling a fish improperly on spinning tackle causes serious line twist. If you continue turning the reel handle without any line coming in, the rotating bail twists the monofilament. On reels with a gear ratio of 5:1, you put five twists in the line for every rotation of the handle. It is vital that you pump the fish on spinning, making certain that line will be recovered when you work the reel.

Fish are lost because of angler error or tackle failure. The longer your adversary is in the water, the greater the chance you will lose it. Picture yourself as a fighter looking for the opportunity to score punches. Conserve energy when you can and pick your moments to slug it out. You can do very little when the fish is at long range. Stretch in the line puts meager pressure on your quarry. If necessary, use the boat to close the distance quickly. The alternative is to work the fish back and forth until it is within 100-feet or so.

Every time you pause or rest, the fish is regaining its strength and getting the proverbial second wind. Too many anglers believe that a bent rod is all the pressure they need to tire a fish. Battles have lingered an hour or more with the fish no more than 50-feet from being landed. It turns broadside to relieve the pressure and the sport on the rod finds himself in a standoff.

The same type of draw occurs when a fish that dove deep hovers at mid-depth, refusing to come topside no matter how much pressure is applied. When that happens, you must continue to try to regain line, relying on very short pumps and quick, half-turns of the reel handle. It's give and take, but the battle goes on.

When a fish is near the surface and turning broadside, applying side pressure can hasten the outcome. If the head of the fish is moving to your right, sweep the rod low and parallel to the water toward the left. Put pressure on the fish and try to turn its head. Once the fish changes position to counter the pressure coming from your left, switch the rod to the right. You're trying to move the fish much as a sailboat would tack into the wind . . . first one way and then the other.

Holding the rod upright when a fish is close, but moving directly away from you seldom leads to a speedy conclusion. Try side pressure and then slip the rod tip in the water. Your goal is to force the fish to turn over. This is a disorienting tactic. It doesn't work all the time, but when it does, the advantage slips back to you.

THE FINAL MOMENTS

With small fish, there's a tendency to reel down and then lift the fish out of the water, trying to swing it aboard the boat. A better solution lies in slipping a net under your quarry. Fish are lost easily when you lift them out of the water. If you are

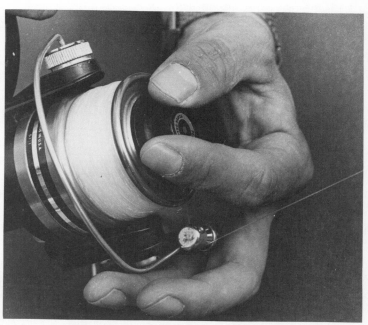

The drag on a spinning reel should be set at about 15 percent of the line's breaking strength. Rarely should one adjust the drag during the battle. Cup the spool to apply extra pressure when needed.

going to net any fish, put the net in the water and lead the fish into it. Keep the net at a 45 degree angle with part of it submerged. Fish cannot swim backward, so their own momentum will carry them into the mesh.

Regardless of size, count on a fish making a final surge near the boat or beach. You know it is going to happen, so be ready. Remember that the least amount of drag on the reel occurs when the rod is pointed directly at the fish. If your adversary surges, drop the rod tip and let the fish swim away. You can bring it back once, twice, three times, or as many as it takes. Trying to snub the fish and hold it alongside the boat leads to broken lines and pulled hooks.

Keep the fish in front of you at all times. If it moves parallel to the boat, walk with it. If it swims under the boat, put your rod in the water and work it around bow or stern until you and the fish are on the same side once more. Side pressure often helps in steering the trophy on the end of your line.

Decide before the final moment whether you intend to release the fish or plan to keep it for dinner. If you are going to turn it loose, restrict handling to a minimum and keep the fish in the water alongside the boat while you remove the hook. A hook disgorger, needle nose pliers, or forceps make the task easier. If you have to hold a fish, use a wet towel or wet gloves to reduce damage to the mucous over a fish's skin. Should the fish be hooked deeply, cut the leader as close to the mouth as possible.

Don't let a fish thrash violently. When necessary, use a net or slip a gaff through the membranes of the lower jaw and hold the fish while you take care of the hook. A growing number of anglers are resorting to tailers that can be eased over the tail of a fish to facilitate handling it without doing any damage. The less a fish is handled, the better its chances for survival. With billfish, you can cut the leader near the mouth and it will swim away unharmed.

If the fish is destined for the table, use a net whenever possible. Gaffing a fish is a bit trickier. Don't make wild swings at the fish. Instead, put the gaff in the water and let the angler swim the fish over the gaff. All you have to do is lift sharply. Be careful that the gaff is not in front of the leader or you could cause a last minute breakoff. It goes without saying that the point of the gaff must be sharp to penetrate. It's also possible to reach across the back of the fish or under the belly. The same striking momentum should help you lift the fish out of the water and into the boat.

Handling a fish can be tricky business, particularly if it has sharp teeth, pointed spines, or it happens to be exceptionally large. Plan the procedure before you attempt it. Wear gloves to help grip your quarry. Open the fish box before you bring it aboard. With species such as wahoo or king mackerel, try to gaff it closer to the head so you can maintain better control. One swipe with those teeth can lay a leg open to the bone.

There's a growing trend toward releasing fish. Before you turn one loose, make sure it has regained its strength and equilibrium. Hold it in the water and move it back and forth until it swims out of your hand. With large fish, hold them alongside the boat and put the boat in gear. Move forward slowly so that water is forced through the fish's gills. It will let you know when it can make it on its own.

Finally, there is little reason to kill sharks and barracuda. Some people feel it is macho to destroy these fish just because they have teeth. A shark can be cut loose easily and barracuda handled without incident.

If you intend to deal with a shark in any way other than cutting the line, do remember that it does not have a bony skeleton and can just about bite its own tail. Grab one carelessly and that shark will have you in an instant. Large ones can be even more dangerous, particularly if you drag them aboard the boat.

Sooner or later, you're going to hook the fish of your dreams. When you do, follow the same rules and procedures for fighting and landing any other fish. If you baby it, there's a good chance the tackle will fail or you'll make a mistake. Instead, slug it out toe to toe and you'll relish the victory when it is all over.

The final moments of the battle are critical. Expect the fish to surge and make a last dash for freedom. When it happens, drop the rod tip and let your quarry go. Trying to snub a fish usually results in a broken line.

LIVE BAITING

Fishing with live bait is a highly effective, yet specialized means of capturing gamefish. In contrast to artificial lures or rigged naturals whose actions are calculated mostly by the angler, boat speed, and sea conditions, the inherent behavior of a live bait suspended in a hostile environment brings out the best in fish. Live bait provides an opportunity for an average angler who has a basic understanding of how and where to fish them to consistently score with quality catches similar to those enjoyed by the more seasoned fishermen. As potent as a live bait may be, there is still quite a bit of skill involved in its presentation. Live bait techniques take many forms, but limited space allows us to review the most popular.

CASTING

Casting a live bait to a gamefish ranks as one of the more exciting forms of fishing. Whether you're pitching a shrimp to a tailing bonefish in the Florida Keys or a live mackerel to a striped marlin off Southern California, the presentation will dictate your success. Move too close to the fish or cast a bait short of the target area and the quarry will depart from the scene, often leaving a violent spraying of white water or marl in its wake.

Southern California and Baja anglers continually pursue striped marlin and broadbill swordfish as the fish tail or bask at the ocean's surface. This form of live bait fishing is so popular that several west coast boat manufacturers locate live wells in the stern and extra wide casting pulpits on the bow of their large sportfishing craft. With a live green mackerel impaled on about a 7/0 or 8/0 short shank hook resting in the well, the captain will either troll lures (plugs) and search for fish at the surface or simply cruise and scan the water for one to bait.

When a fish is spotted, an angler is immediately sent to the bow to prepare for his cast. The captain's job is to monitor the fish's movements, positioning the boat above and slightly to the outside of its path. When the fish is within casting distance, the angler will lob the bait beyond it, retrieving it on an interception course. The bait will be stopped around 15 or 20 feet from the fish. The pickup should be instantaneous if it's hungry, and a short drop-back is allowed before setting the hook.

The advantage an angler has fishing off of a boat's bow lies in the captain's ability to quickly narrow the distance between a hooked fish. This is particularly important on light tackle. When the fish has settled into the depths, the angler can then transfer into the cockpit and receive the full aid of the crew when it comes time to wire the catch. Experienced live bait fishermen have four or five outfits rigged and at the ready, with a second angler designated as backup in case his cast is off target or more than one fish is spotted. Leaders are usually 12 or 15 foot strips of 80 or 125 pound test monofilament, secured to the fishing line with a surgeon's knot.

A similar strategy prevails in the Florida Keys when the winter run of sailfish is underway. In waters as shallow as 15 and 20 feet, sailfish often corral schools of ballyhoo. It's an exciting form of fishing that lets an adept angler select the fish he wants to battle. Naturally, the abundance of a specific bait will likely put the fish into a selective feeding pattern, forcing an angler to obtain a sampling of the baits if he chooses to score.

Utilizing spinning gear with 12 or 20 pound test line, a 7/0 hook and around 10 or 15 feet of 50 or 80 pound test monofilament leader, an angler must cast the bait to the outskirts of a ballyhoo school that has attracted the attention of sailfish. The sails will patrol the outer fringes of the school, with each member taking a turn darting through the pack of bait. They'll quickly charge any fish that strays from the group's sanctuary. The bait will be no exception if it's presented properly.

The water will be clear enough on a calm day to watch a sailfish take the bait. When it does, engage the reel's drag, take up the slack, and strike several times. If a fish becomes suspicious of a bait, due in part to the water's clarity, it may be necessary to re-rig with a 40 or 50 pound test leader and a slightly smaller hook to reduce the prominence of the terminal gear. The hook is always positioned barb first through a ballyhoo's lower jaw, and the shank secured down its beak with copper rigging wire.

Anytime fish are found rounding up bait, whether they're sailfish in Florida, white marlin in the northeast, tarpon, jacks or bluefish on the beaches, always concentrate your fishing efforts on the outskirts of the action. Predatory fish rarely drive through a pod of bait. Instead, they'll keep the members in a tight ball, randomly feeding on those that break stride from the group. They know that by adhering to a pattern, they have a better chance of controlling the bait and are not likely to disperse the school. A live bait cast into the middle of a bait pod will do its best to intermingle for protection. On the outskirts, however, its impeded swimming action, stemming from the hook and leader, will be more readily noticed by a gamefish.

DRIFTING

Drifting is a means of letting a bait develop a somewhat natural rhythm governed by the current and a boat's drift rate. It

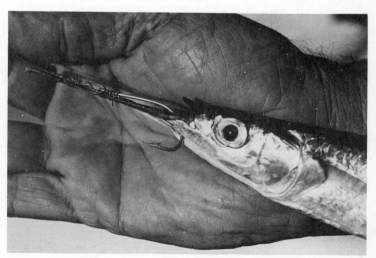

Live ballyhoo make an excellent offshore or inshore bait. Slip a short-shanked hook through the lower jaw and wire the shank of the hook to the bait's bill with soft copper wire.

When fishing live menhaden, veterans often prefer a treble hook rather than a single. One hook goes through the bait's nostrils and the other two await the strike.

Hooking a live mullet back by the anal fin allows the fish to dig deeper in the water. If the mullet is hooked in the lips or in front of the dorsal, it has a tendency to stay shallower.

allows an angler to cover more ground with his baits in the water, increasing the odds of locating fish. Similar to casting, there's an element of skill involved in drifting a livie, such as detecting a bait's distress rate, which often indicates the presence of a predator, and knowing how and when to set the hook.

Drifting techniques can be as simple as fishing a live eel or menhaden for striped bass or as complex as working a kite for billfish. One of the productive elements of a slow drift is the bait's ability to work below the surface. Exactly how deep a bait will run depends on the species and the amount of line tethered out; in most cases, it's not unusual for the penetration to approach 20 feet. When pursuing gamefish that frequent or reside at the bottom, it sometimes becomes necessary to weight a live bait in order for it to reach the productive zone. Striped bass is a prime example. Anglers who share a fondness for chasing these coastal warriors understand that a good

portion of their feeding is done along the bottom and will ri[g] their baits accordingly. With live menhaden, for example, [a] lead weight above the leader may be used to hold the bait nea[r] the bottom in deep sections of a sound. Again, to maintain th[e] action of a bait, use the lightest lead possible to accomplis[h] the task.

Tarpon fishermen working Boca Grande Pass, a dee[p] west Florida inlet that characteristically maintains swift tide[s,] need a considerable amount of lead on a bait that's destine[d] for the bottom. A live mullet or a pinfish is sometimes lowere[d] down with as much as a pound of weight. To see the rig at th[e] dock, it would appear that its intentions are for deep droppin[g] to grouper in waters greater than 300 feet. Yet, the weights ar[e] tied breakaway style with a single strand of soft copper wir[e] and usually fall free on the hook set, leaving the angler and fis[h] to battle it out with no additional burdens.

The same procedure can be used when live baiting mos[t] bottom fish, regardless of how deep the waters are. The trick i[s] to use the least amount of weight that will take a bait dow[n] securing it far enough away from the bait so that it won[']t drastically hamper its action. With the weight at least three [or] four feet above the hook, it will rest on the bottom and th[e] excess line will permit the fish to enticingly swim just above i[t.]

THE DOWNRIGGER

As an increasing number of salt water anglers becom[e] more familiar with the units, the downrigger is proving to be a[n] invaluable tool for live bait fishermen. Their main advantage [is] that they can present a bait at practically any depth without th[e] need of permanent weights. The various tricks and technique[s] used by live bait fishermen are just beginning to surface.

Expert wreck fishermen in the mid Atlantic and south[-] eastern states are using live baits on downriggers with impre[s-] sive results. They'll position themselves up current of a wrec[k] and measure out enough line for the bait to reach the edge [of] the structure. The line will then be fastened to the downrigger clip and lowered to a determined depth. Relying on a boat[']s maneuverability, the bait can be precisely positioned an[d] fished at just about every point on that wreck. Furthermor[e,] the angler always retains the ability to motor away from th[e] structure if he believes the hooked fish has a chance t[o] penetrate it.

Downriggers can be used inshore with equal efficienc[y] trolling live bait along bridge spans or channel edges. In fact, [a] handful of Florida Keys tarpon anglers have been using the[m] in a manner similar to the wreck fishermen, but concentratin[g] around the bottom of bridge spans. With a broad mind an[d] some experimentation, you'll find that a downrigger is appl[i-] cable for most species. Think about it! The next time you'r[e] anchored and live baiting a deep channel or an inlet, wha[t] would happen if a downrigger was used to hold one bait o[n] the bottom while you freelined the others? The spread ca[n] become even more effective under chumming conditions.

The precise tension setting of a quality downrigger cli[p] allows a bait to be released with the slightest tug, for sensitiv[e] fish that require a dropback, or by a firm strike. The outfits hav[e] been used successfully in fooling wary fish, such as sailfish an[d] tarpon, and coincide with other live baiting strategies t[o] effectively cover an entire water column.

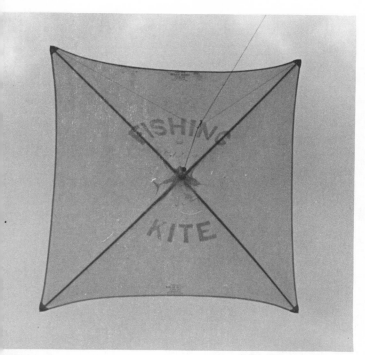

fishing kite expands opportunities for anglers fishing live bait. Originally a blue water tool, the kite is just as valid shore. It keeps a live bait struggling on the surface.

KITE FISHING

In sharp contrast to placing a bait deep, a fishing kite uspends a live bait on the water's surface, where it emits stress signals that are almost irresistible to predators. Developed by the Polynesians and perfected by a handful of U.S. harter captains, the fishing kite is merely a stretch of lightweight cloth over a series of hollow fiberglass supports, forming a square configuration. The density of the cloth and its ame strengths comprise four models: Light wind (up to 10 nots), medium (between 10 and 15 knots), heavy (15 and 20 ots) and extra heavy (between 20 and 25 knots).

The standard kite rig is a short aluminum pole with a ooden reel, although a conventional reel and cut down rod ight be more efficient. It comes spooled with a few hundred feet of 30 or 40 pound test dacron, with a clothes pin riding behind the snap swivel at its opposite end. The general operation calls for a kite to be attached to the snap swivel and tethered out some 50 feet until the clothes pin, sliding down the line in the process, is halted by a tiny swivel. At this point, the actual fishing line carrying the live bait will be placed in the clothes pin. Additional kite line will be spooled out, with the swivel carrying the clothes pin and fishing line away from the boat. During this procedure, a second angler is needed to stop line playout when the bait is not directly under the kite and to continue to free spool the fishing line when the bait is lifted completely out of the water. Once in position, the kite reel's drag is locked down and the bait on the fishing rod is reeled up enough so that its dorsal fin slightly breaks the water's surface. The ensuing commotion is what attracts gamefish.

To truly maximize the kite's effectiveness, some slight modifications are required. The standard clothes pin should be replaced with an outrigger clip that can better handle the chores. With such a clip, particularly the Black's Kite Clip manufactured in Homestead, Florida, the fishing line can be freespooled and reeled up freely. Also, its tension setting can be adjusted to effectively hold a bait regardless of its size, a procedure the standard clothes pin has trouble executing. Furthermore, a second clip can be added to deploy an extra bait. Simply take a drill and bore out the release clip's sleeve enough for it to pass over the small swivel. About 40 or 50 feet behind the first swivel, cut the Dacron and retie it to the ends of a swivel that's just large enough to catch the second clip.

Aside from presenting a bait to a fish in a different manner, a kite provides a means of deploying a series of baits by carrying them off the downwind side of the boat and leaving the opposite gunwale free to organize another spread. For example, a pair of baits can be fished at the surface via the kite, while three baits can be drifted with the current off the opposite side of the boat. One bait can be kept within 10 feet of the surface by tying a balloon just above the leader, another one can be live-lined (drifted freely without any restrictions), while a third bait can be fished deep with a downrigger. You'll soon be able to determine what the most productive depths are.

Baits dangling below a kite need constant attention. The varying wind velocities can raise and lower a kite with regularity, prompting one to constantly take up slack and reposition the bait on the surface, or perhaps lower it back into the water. Upon the strike which can be heartstopping, quickly reel in the fishing line until it falls from the clip and becomes taught before striking the fish. The amount of line falling from the clip is more than a substantial drop back, working perfectly on billfish. Kites also can be deployed while power drifting.

Regarded as a blue water technique aimed primarily at sailfish, the fishing kite can be used on almost all offshore pelagic species with deadly success. And it's by no means restricted to that field. Inshore fishermen can use a kite on tarpon, barracuda and bluefish, with some fresh water bass anglers even employing it to drop live shiners in holes encompassed by dense vegetation that they ordinarily wouldn't be able to get to. Even a surf angler can ferry a bait a great distance seaward and take advantage of species staying just out of casting range, providing he has the wind at his back.

lease clips on a kite must be lightweight or the kite will not properly. There should also be a screw to adjust tension.

POWER DRIFTING

Power drifting is when a boat's forward motion is used to cover ground while trolling a spread of live baits. In contrast to dead-drifting, a boat operator can alter his course to cover various water columns, and hold the boat in a specific area if he believes fish are present. The school-like formation of live baits are strategically positioned behind the transom, depending upon the size of the boat and number of baits fished, and the operator is quickly able to quarter and chase down a fish, without removing the other baits.

Depending on the baits, most are hooked just forward of the dorsal so that they swim in a deep, digging fashion. Offshore anglers generally fish a bait off each outrigger and two from the flat lines. They'll stagger the pack, beginning with a lead fish and ending with a straggler. The throttle will be engaged to prevent the spread from intermingling, and then pulled into neutral to allow them to swim freely. A major mistake made by those using this technique is pulling the baits too quickly. Again, you'll only want to rely on the throttle to separate the baits and to cover slight distances. Baits that are pulled too quickly loose their effectiveness and rapidly drown.

Inshore anglers, with the exception of large boats on sizeable bodies of water, are often geared to handle two outfits. The principle is the same, letting the bait work for you. Inshore anglers going the trolling route should concentrate on structure such as depressions, ledges, and oyster bars, where bait and gamefish are likely to be. Gulf coast anglers searching for trout often slow troll live finger mullet or pinfish along the outskirts of oyster bars and bridges with a reasonable amount of success. Mobile Bay is just one example of a body of water that has turned up many large trout on livies pulled around its structure, especially along the spans of the Dauphin Island Bridge. The experienced anglers often calculate the tides and try to concentrate their efforts on the down current side of flats or oyster bars. They know that fish should be close by feeding on the morsels swept from the shallows, and that their slow trolled live bait will soon be very vulnerable.

A live shrimp is a deadly bait that is in high demand by inshore anglers along the southeastern and gulf coast states. Comprising a major food source of almost all inshore species, live shrimp can be fished in a variety of productive ways. A favorite method of trout fishermen is drifting a live shrimp two or three feet behind a popping cork over grass flats or channel edges. The popping or chugging sound emitted by the cork as it works at regular intervals draws attention to the shrimp which is threaded tail first onto the hook. Aside from trout, this rig will consistently produce redfish, sheepshead, and ladyfish. The technique is also effective when small fin fish or eels are used as bait.

HOOKING THE BAIT

Precisely where to hook a live bait will depend on the species and how it will be fished. Live shrimp, for example, are often hooked through the hard mantle, just forward of the black dot (heart), to maximize their action. However, this arrangement enables small fish to pick away at the morsel, eventually removing it from the hook. If you want to increase a live shrimp's hook up potential, or when casting with one for species such as bonefish, tarpon or redfish, insert the hook

The most common method for hooking live bait is right i front of the dorsal fin, taking care not to put the hook throug the backbone. Smaller and lighter hooks make it easier for th fish to swim.

point first through the tail, threading it through the body an out just below the head. Make certain to remove the tail so won't hamper the action of a shrimp worked through th water. A live shrimp can be fished at or near the bottom b adding a weight just above the leader or impaling a small lea head under and out the top of its mantle.

Live fin fish that will be trolled should be hooked just front of their dorsal fin so that they are pulled slightly dow ward or through the mouth (usually the top jaw on mullet) s their breathing won't be impaired. A bridle rig is sometim used to prevent a hook from burying itself inside a bait. create one, run five or six inches of 20 pound test Dacron li through the fish's upper eye socket with the aid of a riggi needle. Tie the ends of the line together with an overha knot, forming a circle. Tie the circle of line in the middle form two sections, and then hitch the tag end around t hook. The same rig is used to tow bonito, dolphin and sm tuna for blue marlin, though a heavier Dacron is recor mended.

Sandworms and bloodworms can be threaded on single hook and drifted slowly for striped bass or weakfis Eels also can be double hooked by adding a trailer hook to t rig. The second hook is embedded lightly in the mid to low portion of the eel, and is effective in nabbing slashing fish su as bluefish. A live eel can even be sent to the bottom on a sm lead head or metal jig.

Impale a live crab in the corner of the shell with the hook po going from the bottom to the top. If you reverse the hook may hang in the grass when the crab seeks sanctuary.

PREPARATION

Inshore or offshore, successful trolling hinges on a number of important factors ranging from diagnosing the water for signs of fish to the proper baits and their positioning. It's not simply a matter of dragging baits behind the boat and waiting for a fish to strike. Experience dictates the type of bait and how many should be deployed on a given day, how close or how far back they should be fished, and whether they should be riding at the surface or just below it. There's rarely any guesswork involved.

Advanced preparation is critical to a successful outing. Just as one wouldn't head out blindly in the family car on a summer vacation, fishermen have to map out in their minds the different options and routes that can lead to a memorable venture. Anglers who frequently chase migratory species have learned to chart out and monitor the behavior of their favorite fish. By keeping a pulse on fish populations, availability of baitfish in an area, water temperature, wind direction, and strength, they'll have a good idea as to where the species are likely to show up next. The same principles apply to tuna and bluefish in the northeast, the white marlin fishery in the Gulf of Mexico, sailfish and tarpon off South Florida, etc. Predicting with accuracy where and when gamefish will appear takes

years of practice. By learning to communicate with other fishermen along the coast, you should be able to divulge pertinent information as to the whereabouts of fish concentrations, their depths, and estimated arrivals in your area, as long as you return the favor. Learning more about fish migrations and behavior will not only reduce the time it takes to find them, but will ultimately reflect in the quality of your catch.

ON THE SCENE

You'll want to begin your trolling pattern in an area you believe holds fish, watching for any signs that may tip you off to their exact location. If you've worked the area and it seems void of life, it's time to continue the search elsewhere. Inshore and offshore anglers will basically be hunting for similar signs. The bluefish angler trolling inside Chesapeake Bay and the South Florida dolphin fisherman both know that diving birds mean fish. As they scan the horizon, they'll also be paying attention to any rips or tidal changes that may disorient baitfish. Offshore anglers realize that a quality weedline increases their odds of locating fish. A weedline can consist of a wide belt of sargassum that stretches many miles across a sea's surface or scattered patches. These weeds, collectively bonded by wind and currents, serve as a nursery for juvenile

...well-equipped, center-console is a formidable fishing machine. Constantly watching the baits astern becomes an important ...rt of successful trolling.

fish which, in turn, attract larger predators. Anglers scrutinizing a weedline before deploying baits often make the most of valuable fishing time. If a weedline is rich in sea life, it'll be worth fishing. It there are no signs of bait, it's usually best to continue the search for flotsam that is teeming with life.

Acquiring the loran numbers of abrupt drop-offs, wrecks, underwater mountains, ridges or other permanent structures will prove to be invaluable aids in locating fish. Baitfish seek protection and food around such formations and gamefish constantly lurk nearby. Depending upon the species, anglers often base their trolling strategies over these areas. They know that shifts in tide, current or wind direction can have a positive effect on the fishing by washing against these structures and displacing the bait. If loran numbers aren't available, the prominent areas can be pinpointed with some degree of accuracy on a navigational chart. By using a chart recorder and by watching for other boats that may be working in the vicinity, an angler can often zero in on the find. Anglers should always check their graph recorders while pursuing fish, possibly locating concentrations of bait that may be holding within specific depths. The total angler is very cautious not to overrun fish during his flight. Years of experience have taught him to read the entire water column, not just the surface. He knows that by locating the bait, he'll also locate the gamefish.

WORKING A SCHOOL OF BAIT

Properly approaching and working a baitfish school requires a strategy and constant attention. Fish schooling on the surface are leery and anything less than a well thought out approach will send them deep. Warm water anglers realize that schools of small bonito generally attract marlin, sailfish, dolphin, and wahoo. The inept fisherman may anticipate a "gold rush" and charge directly through the pack with trolling baits in order, but an angler with a few years of experience under his belt will try to exploit that school to his advantage. He'll attempt a well-executed pass by the lead fringes of the school, only after he calculates their movements. He'll keep the boat at a distance, generally letting out more line than usual to lessen the chance of disturbing the fish. If the initial pass fails to produce a member of the school, a wide 360 degree pass is executed before repeating the procedure. By being as unobtrusive as possible and working only the outer fringes, the school should stay on top and ultimately the odds of an angler connecting with a fish will improve. An experienced angler can sense fish becoming aware of the boat and will back off as a result, working wider patterns until the surface commotion resumes. The same procedure should be applied to schooling gamefish as well.

Concentrations of bait at or below mid surface depths won't be as gun shy as those on the surface, and a few overhead passes probably won't disturb them. It's still wise to troll along the fringes where the gamefish are likely to be. Once a bait pod is located, an angler should concentrate on raising gamefish to the surface. This can be accomplished by marking the bait and trolling wide, figure eight patterns within the vicinity. If a reasonable amount of time lapses without a strike, it may be necessary to lower a bait into the active region via a downrigger, trolling weight, or by simply disengaging the boat's gear and permitting the offerings to drift down. Lower-

The swimming mullet is a deadly, but often ignored offshor bait. It is rigged with an egg sinker under its chin and troll just below the surface.

ing a jig on either a spinning or bait-casting outfit is also a efficient way to check your chart recorder findings.

Selective feeding is when gamefish devour only a certa species of bait, rendering trolled offerings useless. This ofte occurs when there's an abundance of a specific bait in an are which have been herded into pods by gamefish for feedir purposes. By obtaining several "local" baits and fishing the alive, you'll be able to compensate for this peculiar behavic Baits such as menhaden, mullet or pilchards are best nette while bonito, mackerel and small dolphin can be caught I trolling tiny feathers. The livies can either be slow trolled I bumping a boat's throttle in and out of gear with just enoug speed to keep the lines in a straight fashion, or drifted.

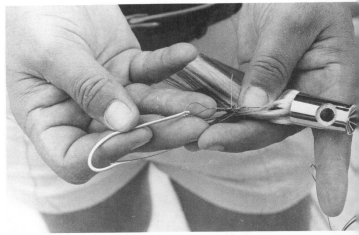

On the offshore grounds, a balao with a feather, skirt, small lure in front ranks as a prime bait for a variety species. A needle-eye hook fits nicely in the throat latch of th balao.

IN THE COCKPIT

Just as a successful angler forms a trolling strategy befc he sets forth in the morning, you can rest assured that his boa cockpit is proficiently laid out. An efficient cockpit is a produ tive one. Layouts vary to some degree, depending upon t boat and sought after species, but they all incorporate a simi principle. Take a quick once-over of a fishing boat's cock and you'll notice that its arena is relatively clean and uncl tered. Naturally, there's not much hope of consistently cate ing fish with the imminent threat of tripping over equipment any hindrances that may snag a fishing line. Even the fisherman in a jon boat that does little else than troll up and down a river will keep certain sections of his skiff clear of obstacles that may reduce his ability to maneuver and play out a fish.

Any coolers, whenever possible, should be removed from the cockpit and stored forward if they're likely to be in the way. Gaffs should be organized and stored in a convenient place, along with a rod harness, fighting belt, and gloves. Ditto docking lines and tackle boxes, even if it means moving most of the equipment forward while fishing.

The inshore boater can do without a fighting chair, but it could be critical to anglers pursuing offshore fish. Even with trolling gear testing between 30 and 50 pounds, there will come a time when a large fish such as a tuna, marlin or shark will test your stamina. A fighting chair used in conjunction with a shoulder harness can reduce fatigue, keeping a fisherman mentally and physically alert to compensate for any last ditch effort that a fish may make. Such a keenness can make the difference between losing or catching the fish.

A chair doesn't have to be expensive to be effective. In fact, many large marlin and tuna have been whipped by anglers using stock chairs with no modifications other than the addition of a gimbal. A fighting chair placed in the bow section of an open boat will enable a captain to run down on a fish, giving him the speed and maneuverability to quickly close the gap between the critter and his angler. A stern mounted chair on an outboard powered boat will require a strong fish to be quartered or backed down upon. The jury is still out as to the most advantageous placement. However, it's worth remembering that when using lines testing no heavier than 50 pound test, an angler can work his way to the bow and stand while the captain pursues a hot fish. Once the fish is under control and it settles into the depths, the angler can then transfer back to the stern chair to finish the battle. By keeping the fish off the stern, the boat handler can properly lead it to the wire man. An angler fighting a large fish from the bow always runs the risk of losing control at boatside.

The optimum number of baits that a crew can effectively handle increases one's chances. While two baits may be easier to manage on a small bay boat, four rods can be fished without the necessity of outriggers on an offshore craft. Two outfits can be fished from the gunwale holders, while another pair can be fished flat and short from a rocket launcher. If there's no central rod placement within the cockpit, the additional outfits can also be fished from the aft gunwale holders. By running the flat lines through a pair of outrigger clips attached to the transom eyes, an angler can reduce their angle of entry into the water. Providing these two baits are fished close to the transom, they will not interfere with the other two fishing lines that run beyond them. The same results are obtainable by securing a clip to a trolling outfit's reel seat, or by restraining the line with a strand of copper wire from the same position.

Boats between 21 and 26 feet rely primarily on outriggers to space fishing lines. Two rods can be fished from the riggers and two outfits worked directly behind the boat. You can possibly sneak in a fifth line from a center rigger mounted to a T-top or from a rocket launcher. However, don't get carried away by how many fishing rods you can put into service. The number of baits that are fished behind a boat should be based on the vessel's size, the availability of anglers who can handle the outfits, the amount of fish within an area, and the weather. If the waters are teeming with fish and strikes are occurring on a regular basis, four rods are sufficient. This is particularly true when fish are found schooling and there are a limited number of hands on board. While it appears likely that you'll increase the harvest of schooling fish by deploying more rods, the efficiency in handling the spread will be reduced and, in the long run, it can cost you fish. Conversely, it may take up to six baits fished in conjunction with a teaser or two to create enough surface commotion when fish strikes are few and far between.

BACK UP GEAR

An effective cockpit also carries an impressive supply of backup gear. Such an assortment can consist of several spinning and bait casting outfits, rigged and at the ready to take advantage of a variety of opportunities. Swimming plugs, jigs, and chuggers (rigged with steel and mono leaders) will pique the interest of most gamefish. Should an angler discover a school of fish, he can place the heavy outfits aside and enjoy some light tackle sport. The advantage of having several rigged outfits at hand is that an angler won't lose valuable time rerigging an outfit, should he break a fish off. A rod rigged for live bait earns its keep aboard most boats. If a billfish is seen tailing down sea, impaling either a live bait or a fresh dead one

A thin rubber band looped around the fishing line and the reel handle lowers the pull on a flat line. It also allows you to keep the reel in freespool with the clicker on for a dropback.

and casting it to the fish will usually get its attention. Keeping fresh fish handy for chumming or baiting will also be advantageous. Trying to cover all the bases takes plenty of devotion and work. However, being ready for that one particular fish that suddenly appears behind the boat will make all the labor worthwhile.

ORGANIZATION

A boat captain is similar to a professional quarterback in that the success of his team will depend on his calls and his players abilities to carry them through. A good captain always stresses organization. He knows that things happen quickly in the cockpit when a trophy fish is hooked up and that there will be little time to search for necessary items. A proper gameplan consists of assigning each angler to a specific rod before they leave the dock, eliminating the look of confusion, or a mad trophy dash to a rod when the line falls from an outrigger clip. Anglers not fighting a fish should be given specific duties, such as clearing the cockpit of remaining lines, taking up the outriggers in case an angler needs to transfer to the bow, wiring, and gaffing a fish. All the roles should be well rehearsed in each individual's mind before the first bait is deployed.

Trolled baits are generally fished in a V-shaped spread, starting with a lead fish and ending with a straggler closely depicting a natural migratory pattern. Gearing the size of the baits or lures to the sought after species is another crucial step in successful offshore trolling. If large tuna or blue marlin are desired, either medium to large naturals or lures should get the nod. If a mixed bag day is more appealing, scale down the baits accordingly, taking into consideration the size of the fish migrating through. The same principle holds true for inshore trolling. If mackerel are averaging two or three pounds, it makes little sense to fish baits or swimming plugs in sizes they would have difficulty attacking, much less ingesting. A big fish can consume a small bait with ease, yet it's a difficult procedure when the roles are reversed. Always use the freshest natural baits possible; they won't tend to wash out as quickly as an old bait and their fresh scent can make it difficult for fish to turn them loose.

The knowledge of exactly how and where to fish baits under a variety of sea conditions comes with experience. When fishing natural baits in a rough ocean, it's often best to position them farther back than you would on a calm day. They'll tend to ride better and not be subject to the whip and jar from the boat's motion. You'll also want to alter the spread a bit. That is, rather than fishing all skipping baits, mix in a swimmer (weighted bait) or two that will be easier for a fish to locate in a whitecapped sea. You can also use transom clips to reduce the line's angle of entry into the water or a downrigger, for precise depth control.

When the ocean is calm, skipping baits with a swimmer mixed in for good measure, are a common choice. The baits also will be fished closer to the transom to create more of a disturbance. Precisely how to stagger a bait spread will depend on the boat's wake, prop wash, and sea conditions. As a general rule, begin the spread with a bait about 15 feet behind the transom just outside of the agitated water, staggering the others between 15 and 20 feet apart. It may take some

experimenting, but you will learn the most productive strik zones behind your boat. And don't be fooled into thinking fish won't come within 15 feet of your transom to eat a bai Blue marlin and sailfish are notorious for their seemingl uninhibited appearances.

Always monitor your baits, making sure they're workin to their fullest potential. Be aware that a spread which work perfectly trolling into a sea, may require slight adjustmen such as reeling in or dropping the baits back several feet whe a change in course occurs. An effective trolling speed wi depend on sea conditions, the boat, and the type of bai being used. Rigged natural baits always perform best betwee five and eight knots. There are several advantages of slowe trolling speeds. You burn considerably less fuel, compared t the speeds required by most artificial lures. You can present bait to a fish in a more realistic manner and the hook-u percentages will be greater. The purist will even go so far as t claim that there's more skill involved in fishing natural bait What with all the rigging, fine tuning and challenge in workin with a bait to hook a fish, he has a worthy argument.

TROLLING LURES

Offshore artificial lures have become immensely popula within the last decade. They offer the angler convenienc simplicity and productivity. Their greatest asset lies in the fa that they need only to be rigged initially, rinsed off after eac use, and stored in the tackle box until the next outing. Gon are the expenses of purchasing fresh natural baits (whe they're available), the headaches involved in storing then and the time it takes to rig them. There's hardly even a need t replace a lure, unless it has been damaged by a tooth predator.

Most offshore trolling lures are designed to perfor properly at speeds between six and 15 knots, with several the cone shaped heads working at speeds up to 18 or 20 knot Because of the swifter speeds possible, anglers benefit b being able to cover more territory during the day than the normally would by pulling natural baits at five or six knot There are three main styles of lures. The Kona or conca heads act as a scoop, giving them a swimming action. The operate best at slower speeds of around eight knots. The fl head design is the most versatile. It requires a range betwee seven and 12 knots to produce a straight tracking action. Th jet heads also run in a straight line. They operate best at speec nearing 20 knots and are usually deployed when there's a va expanse to cover. Similar to natural baits, the Kona or swim ming designs usually work best in rough seas. On a calm da the blunt nose offerings characteristically raise more of racket. Again, experiment with various throttle speeds un you find a productive one.

The degree that color plays in lure fishing can be argue indefinitely. Underwater studies of the color spectrum reve that darker shades, such as black and purple, permeate farthe through cobalt depths, with the reds proving the least visibl Study a concentration of baitfish roaming offshore and you notice their bluish coloration on top, which fades into a silve grayish tint below. Selecting lures representing this protecti coloration scheme may make a difference by appearing mo natural to a predator. This big-game matching the hatch ca

Deep running plugs have become a favorite among trollers working reeflines, wrecks, and even blue water grounds. Carry two or three sizes.

be applied to natural baits as well. If the offshore waters are teeming with flying fish, for example, the extra effort of locating a tackle shop carrying the fish might provide the edge. If they're not readily available, dark colored skirts slipped over similar appearing baits are good substitutes.

Most artificials can be rigged in a variety of ways. Twelve or 15 feet of 300 pound test monofilament leader with two 12/0 hooks, either free swinging or stiff rigged at a 90 degree angle, is the normal set up for pursuing blue marlin and tuna on 50 pound test gear. With 30 pound test gear, substitute 9/0 or 10/0 hooks. Lures in sizes between four and 10 inches are perfect for most offshore fish, and they can be rigged with leaders testing at 125 pounds and a single hook. If there's a problem with toothy fish, try switching over to a number 9 or 0 wire. Twenty or 30 pound test tackle is ideal for battling the mid size blue water warriors.

Natural baits used in conjunction with 20 and 30 pound test tackle are usually rigged with about eight or 12 feet of number 9 or 10 wire leader. The wire eliminates the line stretch that's characteristic of monofilament leaders, and an adequate length of it will guard the actual fishing line against contact by a large or tail wrapped fish. Large mackerel, squid or mullet have been used with leaders as heavy as number 15 and as long as 15 feet for blue marlin and tuna. The disadvantage of wire leader is that the lighter strands have a tendency to kink at high speeds or on an acrobatic fish. Fish are also less likely to notice monofilament leaders when they are zeroing in on a bait.

Inshore trollers don't have to be as generous with their terminal tackle. They know that bluefish and mackerel will require a small trace of wire to protect their fishing lines, while other species can be captured on monofilament leaders. The lures most often selected for inshore work include swimming plugs, mops, spoons, and chuggers. Depending upon the current and boat speed, it may take some fine tuning to perfect the action of a swimming plug. This can be accomplished by slightly bending the eye ring until a desired action is achieved. It's also important not to snug a knot against a lure's eye ring as it will only impede its action. Furthermore, the larger swimming plugs and spoons have been used by offshore anglers

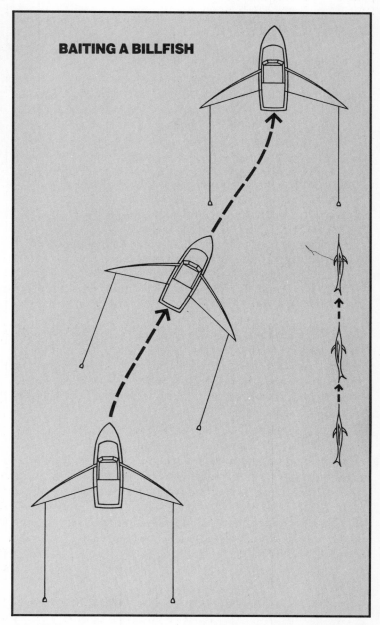

BAITING A BILLFISH

A billfish is spotted on the surface moving down sea. Adjust speed so the boat moves slightly faster than the fish, but remains parallel to it. Once the boat passes the target, ease the helm toward the quarry, allowing an outrigger bait to swing in front of the fish. A slight speed adjustment may be necessary to let the billfish overtake the bait.

A fighting chair makes a difference when battling a husky, stubborn fish. Transom doors on larger boats eliminate the need to hoist a heavyweight over the gunwale.

Water temperature is the single most important factor in determining where fish will be. Carry a thermometer.

with a great deal of success, particularly on kingfish an wahoo. The plugs are slow trolled below the surface with th aid of a trolling sinker or downrigger using about six feet o wire leader. The pulsating action of the bait goes almos unnoticed by fish. Swimming plugs require a slower trollin speed than other types of natural bait, therefore resulting i extra fuel savings.

Whatever the choice may be, there's no substitute fo quality terminal tackle. All hooks should be honed to perfec tion and trolling swivels should be ball bearing in design t prevent line twist. Continually check leaders for frays or nick replacing any that are questionable. And by all means, mak sure your baits and lures are rigged well in advance of a tri Enough time will be spent in locating fish when you leave th dock. Trolling lures, plugs, and extra rigs can be prepared on weekend and stored almost indefinitely in a tackle box. Nat ral baits should be rigged and brined at least a day prior to trip. By layering rows of bait, ice, and coarse salt in a 48 qua cooler, a freezing brine will be created as the mix melts. E adding ice and salt and by draining excess water, baits can b kept fresh upwards of a week. However, make sure to place th leaders between sheets of newspaper or aluminum foil, t prevent them from sticking to the ice and possibly kinking.

THE FIGHT

The strike of most inshore and offshore fish will b sudden, telegraphed by an arching rod and a singing drag. I most cases, an angler need only to pick up the outfit, set th hook, and play the fish out. Enter the billfish. Depending o the bait, billfish have a tendency to first slash or strike a offering with their bill, waiting for the disabled fish to drift bac before consuming it. The only noticeable exception lies wit high speed lures, which they will charge aggressively. Spottin the fish before the strike is a great advantage and a majo reason why a bait spread should be watched ever so close After the initial strike, an angler must freespool the bait to th fish, lightly thumbing the spool to prevent a backlash and t keep the fish from feeling any tension. When he believes th fish has had enough time to consume the bait, the angler w engage the drag, reel up the slack line, and set the hook. He know instantly if it's a solid hook up. Should he miss the fish o the first attempt, all is not lost. The bait should be reeled bac into position for another opportunity. If the fish didn't feel th hook, chances are it'll charge back within seconds.

An effective drop back can even be used on king mackerel, bluefish, dolphin, etc.. Should a fish slash a bait an miss the hook, the remaining portion can be dropped back f several seconds, then slowly jigged back to the surface. Som times, the results are surprising. In most cases, a large fish w require all remaining lines to be brought in and the cockp cleared to give an angler full advantage. Otherwise, it ma prove worthwhile to let the other baits settle into the dept while a fish is being played out. If there are any follower there's a strong possibility that another outfit will soon b singing.

Once the fish is tired, the wire man will take a wrap or tw and lead the trophy alongside the boat. It is here where the fis will be admired and the decision made whether to boat release it.

FISHING A CHUM SLICK

Nothing attracts fish faster or turns them on more effectively than a steady stream of tidbits carefully and systematically tossed over the side. The theory of chumming centers on the ability and willingness of fish to track prey through their sense of smell. Scientists realize that fish discern and distinguish thousands of odors readily, but how they do it remains cloaked in mystery. It's a neat trick when you consider that the odor is masked in water and significantly diluted by this medium.

Techniques may vary along different sectors of coastline, but few species can resist the tempting morsels that telegraph a free lunch. Chumming not only entices one's quarry within range, but the taste of food stimulates their desire to feed and makes them more aggressive. Competition from schoolmates often causes individual members to lose their natural wariness and strike without hesitation.

THREE RULES

Successful chumming depends on three basic rules. When you decide to chum, select an area of known fish concentrations or where gamefish pass on a regular basis. No matter how much skill you exhibit, it's impossible to produce fish in a slick when there aren't any around.

Selecting the right chum holds the key to the second rule. Anything you put in the water should be the best available and must be tailored to the tastes of the species you seek. Round up, oily fish such as menhaden or mackerel make an excellent chum because the fish oils permeate the water and create a slick that often extends several hundred yards down current. You have the option of using more than one offering in combination and it often makes sense to sweeten the slick with other goodies.

The third rule stipulates that a tide or current should be running to broadcast the chum or at least the odor over as wide an area as possible. Position the boat carefully to reap the maximum benefit from the water flow. If you are fishing a wreck, coral head, reef, tower, underwater ledge, or any other form of structure, stay upcurrent from the target so that the chum will filter back to the fish.

MAINTAINING THE SLICK

Once you start to chum, maintaining the slick at a steady rate of flow becomes imperative. Fish exhibit very short attention spans and they quickly disperse once the handouts stop. Even when all hands are busily fighting fish, one person on board must be responsible for keeping the slick going without interruption. Where the situation warrants, put a frozen block of chum in a mesh bag and hang it over the side as the basis of the slick. Water action softens particles and they drift away on a continuous basis. Periodically, it may be necessary to shake the bag. When freshly ground chum is available, one trick is to turn the pail of chum upside down in a plastic milk case. The holes in the plastic case allow the chum to wash away slowly and steadily.

Veterans disagree on the amount and frequency of the chum. Some insist that one should produce a relatively heavy slick to attract the fish and then slow it down when the quarry appears. Others prefer to dilute the chum and ease it out slowly. As a rule of thumb, when one batch of chum drifts out of sight, it's time for the next handful, ladle, or shake of the bag.

ANCHOR OR DRIFT

When fish are concentrated around particular structure, anchoring upcurrent becomes essential so that a steady

Fresh chum and maintaining a steady slick hold the keys to success. When one ladle of chum drifts out of sight, it's time for the next ladle.

stream of chum works back toward the fish. If you are attempting to lure bonefish within casting range, the trick lies in staking out in front of a white patch where you can see the fish more easily. Select a spot where the odor drifts out to a channel or across an area of shallows where bonefish will pass.

Along crowded parts of the coast such as the northeast, anchoring for bluefish is a necessity. There are so many boats in the fleet that a drifting craft would quickly become a menace to everyone else. If you are not plagued by the presence of other boats and the terrain as well as weather conditions lend themselves to drifting, it's worth a try. Most shark chummers anchor, but some do very well drifting.

Deep water eliminates the need to make a decision. On the West Coast, albacore and yellowtail boats toss live anchovies in the water to hold a school of fish. The standard technique lies in drifting because of water depth and the need to get the chum in the water immediately when the school is located. Canyon runners on the East Coast may carry enough anchor line to reach the bottom. If they don't, drift chumming provides the alternative. In Bermuda waters where Argus and Challenger Banks rise from the depths, the preferred practice is to put the anchor on the shallower edge of the bank and let the boat swing back over the deep. The same technique works whenever structure rises from the ocean floor.

CHUMMING SITUATIONS

The limitations on chumming center on desire and imagination. It's a valuable method for catching bait and equally effective in luring gamefish. Once an angler understands the mechanics and believes in the system, he'll engage in chumming at every opportunity.

Along the northeast coast, mackerel and bluefish respond well to chum. Ground menhaden is the standard, but it pays to sweeten the slick with killies, spearing, sand eels, or whatever else happens to be at hand. When bonito invade the slicks in late summer, spearing or sand eels fished with a light leader will fool these fussy feeders. Fresh chum usually produces better results than frozen offerings thawed by sea water.

Tuna chummers rely on chunks to toll in their target. Menhaden, butterfish, and mackerel are excellent choices. These fish should be sliced in chunks about one-half inch to one-inch wide and tossed overboard. The same system works on sharks along this part of the coast. Veterans often use ground up chum along with the chunks to produce an impressive slick, but the chunks alone will work well. A few sharkers rely on chicken entrails and waste products from slaughterhouses.

Sharks can be chummed almost anywhere and the methods vary. In the shallows of the Florida Keys, guides fillet a barracuda and hang it off the side of the boat. There is something about the odor permeating from a cuda that sings a siren's song to sharks. Baiting is done with a chunk of barracuda or artificial lures may be cast once the shark comes within range.

Schools of dolphin will hang around a boat if chunks of balao or mullet are tossed over. Glass minnows, pilchards, Spanish sardines, or similar baits quickly get the attention of the pack and the dolphin linger for more handouts. Even if y[ou] are trolling for dolphin, keep some simple chum ready i[n] cooler. The instant you get a hookup, start chumming and t[he] school should stay with you.

Tarpon have been elevated to a glamour status by t[he] flyrod enthusiast and other proponents of artificial lures, b[ut] they are efficient scavengers. A fresh mullet head fished [on] the bottom often produces results when other methods fail [If] there are tarpon around, cut up chunks of mullet, spot, [and] other small fish and salt the area. Then, cut a bait in half a[nd] put a hook in the head or tail section. Let it lie on the bott[om] and you can almost count on a tarpon picking it up.

Key West Harbor has become a center for chummi[ng] tarpon with shrimp heads or the unwanted fish and crustac[ea] taken in nets by shrimpers. The same method works in oth[er] places where tarpon abound. Bait can be drifted back in t[he] slick or tethered to a lead-headed jig and kept just off t[he] bottom.

This same chum does wonders over wrecks and ree[fs] attracting a variety of species that range from cobia a[nd] amberjack to grouper, snapper, king mackerel, bonito, a[nd] tuna. It's messy work handling this chum, but the results [far] outweigh any discomfort.

When a shrimp boat anchors at first light to separate [the] catch and shovel the net leavings over the side, gamef[ish] congregate. Instinctively, these fish know that breakfas[t is] about to be served. Many shrimpers will allow you to tie aste[rn] of them and fish, frequently saving chum for anglers. A c[old] six-pack or two of their favorite beverage provides a marvel[ous]

Frozen blocks of chum placed in mesh bags and hung o[ver] the side will attract fish. Many tackle shops carry the blo[cks] or you can freeze your own in milk cartons.

...ut up shrimp tossed out on a flat lures bonefish within ...sting range. Tear the shrimp into small pieces rather than ...ce it. The jagged edges give off more scent.

...troduction and quickly establishes a friendly relationship.

Atop the reefs and coral heads, try a mixture of ground ...um and pilchards, glass minnows, squid, and boiled mac-...oni. Yellowtail, mangrove snapper, mackerel, blue runners, ...d a dozen other species will feast on the goodies. You can ...ift baits back or fish the bottom and do equally well.

On the offshore grounds, live bait used as chum pro-...ces exciting results. West coast anglers toss handfuls of ...rdines or anchovies at yellowtail and albacore to hold the ...hools while anglers fish live bait or artificials. Across the ...ntinent on the east coast, live pilchards tempt sailfish, ...berjack, dolphin, and other denizens.

Sometimes, there is a chain reaction. A chum line lures ...e smaller fish and the larger predators, hearing the feeding ...progress, arrive on the scene to investigate. No matter what ...e sequence, the opportunity remains the same.

Coastal anglers often find it necessary to catch live bait ...d chum usually proves to be an invaluable ally. Balao ...spond well to a chum slick and so do blue runners. An ...sortment of bait species may move in to feed once the scent ...d taste of chum reaches them. One then has the option of ...ssing a cast net or catching the bait on rod and reel.

Almost a half century ago, a few skippers discovered that ...nefish responded to pieces of fresh shrimp tossed out as ...um. The technique has been refined in recent years by ...acing the chum on a patch of white sand where anglers ...ned with polarized sunglasses could actually see the fish. ...prevent box fish and other bait stealers from picking up the ...bits, some veterans use a piece of PVC tubing with caps on ...th ends and holes drilled in the pipe. They fill the tube with ...ces of shrimp and position it on the flat. The odor is carried ... the current and it will attract bonefish, although the gray ...ost seldom lingers as it would if it were finding pieces of ...rimp on the bottom.

TYPES OF CHUM

Fish tend to be opportunistic feeders, taking advantage ...whatever food happens to be available. They have the ability to find a meal through their sense of smell just as easily as by sight. Chum that permeates the water faster and more thoroughly frequently tolls in fish faster and with greater effectiveness than other types. Almost any natural food source may be used along with certain human foods and some artificial chums. Packaged fish scents sprayed on the water's surface or mixed in with the chum may help in some situations. It is doubtful they will have a negative effect.

There is considerable evidence suggesting that the fresher the chum, the better it will perform. That is not to say that frozen chum won't do the job, but there are times when the condition of the chum does make a difference. Whether it is fresh or frozen, make an effort to keep it out of the sun and store it on ice until you are ready to use it.

Whenever possible, carry more than one type of chum. Frozen blocks of ground chum or fresh buckets of it offer the perfect place to start. Oily fish such as mackerel or menhaden do a nice job, but you can package your own chum by grinding up the remains of fish after fillets have been removed. This can be mixed with a little water and frozen in milk cartons. Many tackle shops sell frozen blocks if making your own doesn't appeal to you.

A store that stocks bait can provide several different offerings depending on time of year, location, and the type of anglers to which the business caters. In addition to mackerel and menhaden, look for mullet, balao, squid, pilchards, killies, spearing, sand eels, sardines, anchovies, and glass minnows. On the east coast, clams such as skimmers or soft shells are crushed and used as chum for striped bass, weakfish, and other species.

Chumming with grass shrimp for weakfish and stripers is an old, but deadly method along a jetty or in an inlet on outgoing tide. Flounder can be enticed with kernels of canned corn, while certain reef fishes respond to macaroni. Shrimp heads from a processing house work and, of course, the net discards from a shrimp boat rank at the top of the list off some parts of the coast.

The key lies in establishing a basic slick and then sweetening it with other goodies that provide excitement and a mixture of smells. Take enough chum to last as long as you plan to fish. Nothing is more frustrating than to run out of chum just when the action is at its peak.

In deeper water when fish may be hugging the bottom, there are several tricks to draw them topside. Try mixing sand with the chum. The grains of sand help the chum to sink more rapidly. A few experts build a small, metal container with a simple trip mechanism. Sinkers take the container to the bottom and it is overturned by pulling on a line. The next load of chum is tripped a little higher in the water column and so forth.

FISHING A CHUM SLICK

As the current carries the chum away from the boat, it will begin to sink. The trail follows an inclined plane from the boat to the bottom. How fast it sinks depends on the flow of water and the type of chum. Fish that find the slick will follow it toward its source, but in some situations, this could take time. That means that the first fish may be well back in the slick.

Depending on the species one seeks and the tackle

choice, fishing follows two basic techniques. If the water is relatively clear and the fish have a tendency to show in the slick, you can wait until you see them before putting a bait in the water or casting an artificial. When favorable conditions exist, one can actually select the fish before the presentation is made. Bait or lure is simply cast in front of a specific fish.

In this type of fishing, it pays to rig several rods with a choice of lures plus one or two with hooks for natural bait. If the fish remain relatively deep, you may need a leadheaded jig to reach them. As they feed closer to the surface, lighter weight artificials will produce results. At times, lures may be turned down and only natural bait will score. The ability to shift gears quickly by picking up another rod rigged differently frequently helps one to take advantage of the situation when the fish suddenly show.

Drifting a bait blindly in a chum slick requires concentration and practice. There are instances when the fish are swarming around the boat and will strike anything dropped in the water, but an equal number of occasions demand peak performance. The fish tend to remain on the inclined plane that represents the path of the chum. It is essential that your bait follow this lane as closely as possible. That means that it must float freely so that the current will carry it away at the same rate.

Start by stripping off three or four rod lengths of line, allowing it to fall on the surface of the water. Watch it closely. Just before it comes tight, strip more line off the reel and let it fall on the surface. The key lies in maintaining just enough slack so the line never comes tight, but not so much slack that you cannot detect a pickup. When a fish grabs a bait, you'll actually see the line start to move off at a faster rate than the current was carrying it.

If you allow the line to come tight or even pause, the bait begins to rise above the track of the chum and you may be out of the pay zone. When you first start chumming, swim the baits well back in the slick. If nothing happens, reel in and start ove As a rule, use the lightest leader material possible and a sma hook size. When the current begins to wane, shift to sm hooks, light leaders, and relatively tiny pieces of bait. It's a tri that often does the job when standard techniques fail.

Fish working a slick become accustomed to picking u free floating tidbits. There are situations when predato ignore an artificial lure being retrieved through the are preferring to concentrate on the handouts. If you are dete mined to use flies or artificials, let them drift with the chu Plastic imitations of baits are an excellent choice for spinni or plug casting enthusiasts. Fly fishermen should select pattern that gives off the flash of the chum. Swim the ba without imparting any action and you should get a pickup.

With natural baits, change the offering after a strike if it mashed or crushed in any way. Settling for less than the be bait borders on folly. Fish can be very fussy in a slick and i not worth the time to find out by fishing unappetizing baits.

If you think your offering is drifting above the chu attach a small split shot or wrap on sinker and try th approach for a few minutes. Keep watching the slick from th stern of the boat to as far as you can see. When the fish seem be hanging way back and occasionally boiling on the surfac use casting tackle to get a bait back there. You have to go wi the flow and adjust your methods to handle the situation.

Casting is also the answer off the California coast whe live bait is tossed to ravaging schools of albacore or yellowta Flip the anchovy or sardine as far from the boat as possible. it tries to find sanctuary under the hull, a predator should rur down and devour it.

Chumming ranks as one of the most effective anglin techniques with unparalleled potential. It's one that yo should learn thoroughly and practice frequently. From blu fish to bluefin tuna, bonefish to bull sharks, there is no bett way to toll in your quarry and hold them there.

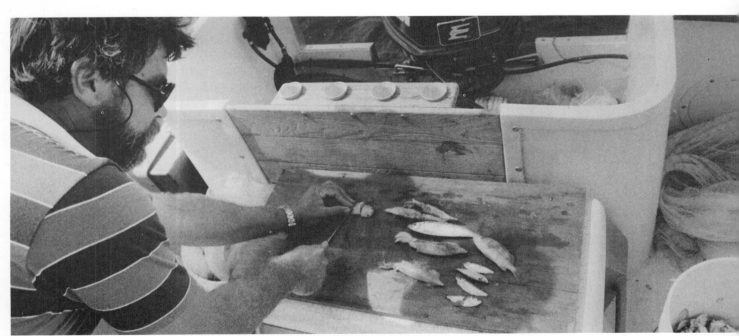

An assortment of fresh bait prepared carefully increases one's chances when bottom fishing or chumming. The right bait mak a difference.

THE GREAT PRETENDERS

The concept of artificial lure fishing probably has roots tracing back to when man first snaked a jagged edged stone through the water in search of fish for survival, not knowing that his rude, yet efficient means of producing food would blossom into a highly popular sportfishing technique. Stalking or searching for fish, then trying to convince them to take a piece of hardware that resembles their natural forage, is an art that most fishermen yearn to master. The degree artificial lures play in fishing depends on the species of fish sought, an angler's skill level, and the degree of difficulty in procuring natural baits.

Artificials are at home practically anywhere there's water and fish. Sizes range from the tiniest of flies used in brackish estuaries to big game trolling lures weighing in excess of two pounds. They can be specialized to target certain species of fish under particular conditions or versatile enough to be effective over a wide range of applications. To maximize his odds of catching fish, an angler must understand the various styles of lures and stock his tackle box with an ample supply of them. Successful anglers realize that a productive day on the water may require a comprehensive investigation of a water column. Lacking a specific lure that'll reach the fish will surely reflect in his catch.

THE LEAD HEADS

Considered to be a most effective addition to any tackle box, the lead head jig is versatile enough to produce fish in a number of situations. It's so adaptable that it commands a permanent ride in military survival kits. It is noted mainly for its ability to penetrate water columns. As its name implies, molten lead is cast into a mold encompassing a hook. After the jig is cast and removed, it will undergo an enamel coating, usually white or yellow, and dressing with wisps of bucktail (expensive versions) or nylon. Many models even include reflective strips of mylar. The end result is a somewhat attractive, yet highly potent lure that sells for considerably less than other forms of artificials.

What makes the jig so effective is its compact size, which is relatively easy for a fish to engulf in a single bite. Unlike swimming lures that contain an inherent action, the lead head's attractiveness depends largely on an angler's experience. If he has a basic understanding of the fish he's pursuing and its feeding habits, he can choreograph the jig's action accordingly.

Redfish and bonefish, for example, are basically bottom feeders. Their underlying mouths enable them to effortlessly ferret out crabs and shrimp from soft terrain. By matching a jig to the size of their local forage and working it in a crawling, burrowing-like fashion, you'll stand a much better chance of attracting a fish's attention. Understand, too, that fish encountered in skinny water will be very wary compared to those in the depths. A proper bait presentation calls for a cast to be made well beyond the fish, with the lure retrieved across the fish's path. A lead head plopped in the water right next to the fish will send it and any others scurrying for the depths.

In channels or along deep drop offs where weakfish, snook or striped bass are apt to frequent, allow the jig to sink before retrieving it. With short sweeps of the rod, hop the jig off the bottom. Such fish will be feeding on shrimp or assorted baitfish swept with the current and you'll want your offering to closely imitate a disturbed action. A chart recorder is instrumental in revealing what portion of the water column the fish are holding in. However, if a certain water column fails to produce a strike, alter the lead head's retrieval, focusing on other zones until you find a productive one. Also, be aware of the surrounding water. If fish are occasionally popping at the surface, try working a jig on top.

Benthic fish such as groupers, sea bass or snappers require a more defined approach. Since these fish rarely venture far from their lairs, it's imperative that a lead head's action be concentrated at or near the bottom. Again, short, hopping movements will yield the best results. In contrast to inshore waters where there's a limited amount of current, offshore jiggers are often faced with swift currents and deep waters. Trying to reach a productive structure in 180 feet of water requires a heavier lead to compensate against any line planing that may result from a swift current. To be effective, a jig must weigh enough to remain on or near the bottom through a series of probes. Furthermore, a fishing line with a direct angle to the bottom will provide an angler with more sensitivity. Jigs that are highly susceptible to currents, planing as they descend, are often rendered ineffective.

While a lead head's action is primarily controlled by an angler, it does have a certain inherent behavior. The lima bean style or those with compressed sides have a fluttering action that can pass for an injured baitfish. If one were to visualize the jig being swept off the bottom several feet, then allowed to

800

Weighted spoons, diamond jigs, and bucktails account for their share of striped bass. These heavy artificials scout the entire water column from bottom to top.

freely drift back down, the fall would be somewhat regulated. A similar sweep with a bullet or straight taper design would produce an immediate and accurate dash towards bottom. The streamlined design of the latter is more effective in penetrating deep waters with minimal interference from current. The former, with its expanded surface area, will not cut as precisely through the water.

Tipping a jig is another way of increasing its potency. Trout anglers are one group of fishermen who realize the extra fish appeal of a jig or bucktail that carries a piece of natural bait. Fish strongly depend on their sense of smell and the slightest trace of food may often be enough to trigger their feeding instincts. If the plain lead head isn't drawing its share of strikes, experiment by adding something natural to it. However, be certain to use a fish or crustacean that's common to the environment to maximize the combination's effectiveness. A jig can even be used as a sinker to hold a bait on the bottom. This method of baiting fish is particularly effective on grouper, sea bass, tarpon, cobia, and a host of other bottom feeders. Key West fishermen are fond of hooking a mojarra or pinfish to a jig, casting it out, and letting it sit on the bottom as they chum over rock piles for grouper and snapper. The chum draws the fish close enough to where they generally discover the bait. Often dubbed the lazy man's technique, a bait/lead head combination doesn't need to be worked to produce a strike.

Pelagic species such as bonito, mackerel, barracuda, kingfish, dolphin and wahoo are willing strikers of fast moving jigs. While these fish can be singled out and cast to, particularly when dolphin and mackerel are schooling, they are mostly surprise catches made by those jigging for bottom fish at or near deep drop offs. Before embarking on any trip, pack a casting rod or two rigged with a bucktail, and take the time to investigate any surface activity.

VERSATILE LURES

Comprising this group are any lures that, like the leadhead, can be used in a variety of situations ranging from inshore to offshore. Among the most popular items are spoons and swimming plugs. Designed with a diamond-like shape and a chrome or highly reflective finish, a spoon closely imitates a distressed baitfish. Similar to the leadheads, the spoons come in many sizes and weights. There are models for casting, deep jigging and trolling. Most designs consist of a single fixed hook, although treble hooks come on some casting models.

The casting spoons can be retrieved steadily within a water column, relying on its built in action, or worked in a manner similar to a leadhead. In fact, there are even small diamond head models that are commonly tipped with bait. These are usually drifted or worked slowly over the bottom where they'll take fish such as weakfish and striped bass. The deep jigging spoons are used to penetrate depths to reach bottom dwellers such as hake or groupers. The shiny flash of the offering also can draw strikes from kingfish, barracuda, wahoo, and other pelagics.

Trolling spoons offer a more consistent, dished-out shape. They usually have a fixed single hook that often determines its size and species designation. The effectiveness of a trolling spoon can be traced to its pulsating motion through

The head shape and weight of a leadheaded bucktail determine its action and sink rate. Use the lightest weight possible under the conditions.

the water, which omits vibrations that are discernible to fish. Add to that the light reflections and it's little wonder why this instrument still holds a place in the tackle lockers of salt water trollers.

The trolling spoon is equally at home inshore or offshore. Anglers searching for bluefish, weakfish or mackerel may do best with models containing hook sizes of a 3/0 or less. Small barracuda, redfish or cobia may be easier to hook on spoons with 3/0 through 6/0 hooks, while offshore anglers will do best with sizes 6/0 and up. In contrast to other trolling baits or lures, usually only one or two spoons are deployed in a spread. Gulf, southern, and mid Atlantic fishermen often mix in a trolling spoon with their regular arrangement of baits when they're working over reefs for kingfish. The radical tracking movements of the lure hardly goes unnoticed by fish, and it seems that the most consistent action occurs within 20 feet of the surface.

While a spoon can be trolled straight off a conventional outfit, they're generally used in conjunction with a planer, downrigger, or wire line outfit to add additional depth. Some success is attainable by attaching a trolling weight between

Japanese feathers have been around forever and they are still one of the most productive trolling lures. Regardless of the spread, fish one short in the wake and it should account for a variety of fish.

When you find a bucktail shape that proves effective for you, carry it in several weights for a variety of situations. Shiny mylar or other flashy material adds more appeal. It can always be removed by simply cutting it off or pulling it out.

the leader and the regular fishing line, but the free swinging weight is often cumbersome to handle. With a downrigger, you can easily vary the depths. Try working a spoon at different levels until you get a strike. If you're fishing two spoons over a reef, try to work one several feet off the bottom for benthic species and the other one at a mid-depth range. Blue water anglers also will find that a spoon fished well below the surface will be effective on wahoo and tuna, particularly during the heat of summer when increasing water temperatures keep the fish down. Like all trolling baits, it's imperative to use a quality snap swivel on a spoon to prevent line twist. Some spoons come with a built in swivel. For those that don't, make certain to place one between the leader and fishing line.

PLUGS AND SWIMMING LURES

There's hardly anything more exciting in the world of fishing than watching a snook, striped bass, or bluefish explode on a surface plug. That's why great numbers of sportfishermen cherish top water lures and expend considerable energy in stalking major gamefish with them. Constructed mostly out of hard plastic or balsa wood in varying sizes and armed with treble hooks, surface plugs and swimming lures depict natural baits more closely than most other forms of artificials.

The chuggers are floating models that feature hollowed out cavities. When they are worked across the surface, water and air become trapped within the cavity, resulting in a popping sound. This noise, combined with the lure's irregular action, sends a distress signal out to fish. Their effectiveness ranges from shallow estuaries for snook or striped bass, surf for bluefish or barracuda, and offshore for bonito, dolphin and possibly sailfish. Key West guides who consistently fish the wrecks in the Gulf of Mexico rely on large chuggers worked erratically over structures between 40 and 70 feet deep to lure amberjack and cobia to the surface. Anglers on the Pacific coast of Panama and Costa Rica religiously fish them for cubera snapper, roosterfish, and sailfish.

Fishing techniques vary, but you'll want to closely imitate baitfish in distress. Depending on where you're fishing, try to coordinate the lure's size with the bait that the gamefish seem to be feeding on. If trout or snapper blues are the quarry, use a lure that will be easy for them to consume. Small chuggers used on slick calm waters are often a better choice than large ones, since they won't emit a loud sound from which wary fish may shy away. Realize, too, that under choppy or rough conditions, it may take the more audible sound of a large chugger to draw attention to it.

Aiming at the targeted spot, cast the lure out and allow it to settle for several seconds. Once the ripples have just about dissipated, start a slow and steady retrieval, pumping the rod on just about every third turn of the reel. The technique can be varied, with the lure being popped at two or three second intervals. Speed and action will depend largely on the species of fish and their aggressiveness on that particular day. Trout anglers prefer a subtle popping pattern, while a loud and radical action is more conducive to exciting amberjack and roosterfish. It'll take a few encounters with fish to figure out the right combination. Once you're locked in, continue the style until conditions dictate a change. Despite occasional feeding blitzes, most surface chuggers are effective in the morning, late afternoon, and evening hours. As fish move deep throughout the day, the lures will not produce as well.

Swimming lures also are designed to imitate an injured baitfish. They'll raise a commotion when worked at the surface almost as much as the chuggers, yet are more versatile because they can cover a greater percentage of a water column. These life-like lures come in sizes of only a few inches upwards to heavy duty offshore models exceeding 15 inches. Those with a protruding lip have a built-in action that can be activated by little more than a steady retrieve. However, slowly twitching the lure with regulated pauses is a proven pattern with many species. They can be retrieved quickly or trolled behind a boat, enticing fish such as jacks, bonito, mackerel, and barracuda.

For most shallow water casting applications or when fish are at or near the surface, the standard lightweight models are a good bet. Similar to chuggers, the effectiveness of a swimming plug often hinges on how well it matches the local bait. Since most fish tend to go on a selective feeding pattern when there's an abundance of a specific bait, an angler must be prepared to pattern his offering accordingly. By casting a lure that resembles the local baitfish and by fishing it on the outskirts of the school, a predatory fish will be more apt to notice it, particularly if it appears lethargic.

Fish that leave the shallows or those that are confined to the depths of channels, ledges, or other submerged structures, often ignore plugs that aren't fished in their territory. Depending upon the water depth, most inshore and sound fishermen can alter a plug's retrieve to do the job. By adding a split shot or two of lead just inches in front of a swimming plug, a fisherman can take a floater to a greater depth. Furthermore, there are weighted models on the market that'll sink until the fisherman begins winding line, and versions that feature an extra long lip to force the body downward. Like all plugs in this category, they can be cast or trolled.

Reaching inshore fish at or near the bottom in waters less than 20 feet deep can be achieved in two primary ways. A small trolling sinker separating the fishing line from the leader or a downrigger can be used to lower a swimming plug into a productive depth, if the extended lip of a deep diver is not sufficient. By playing out a fair amount of line and by keeping the rod tip aimed down at the water, a deep diving lure can be trolled slowly and exceed depths of 15 feet. With a sinking plug, disengaging the boat's throttles at regular intervals should help govern its depth.

The productivity of the swimming lure on the offshore fishing grounds has just begun to catch on within the past few years. Compared to natural baits, they are convenient to obtain, rig and store; require a slower, more fuel efficient trolling speed; and are just plain effective on fish. The large plugs between eight and 14 inches are usually selected for blue water duty, since they have extra strength double or treble hooks to withstand the pressure of heavy tackle. Like the trolling spoon, they seem more productive below the surface. Trolling weights are often used to take a lure down to a productive area. Such weights range from a few ounces on up to a pound, and are usually positioned far enough in front of the plug so they won't hinder its action.

Kingfish are a common target of southeast and Gulf of Mexico fishermen who pull plugs over reefs, wrecks, drop-offs and around oil rigs. In addition to the kings, bonito and an occasional cobia fall for the lures. Grouper fishermen working the South Florida coast and the Florida Keys are enjoying outstanding results fishing these plugs off downriggers. They'll position the offering so that it rides several feet off the bottom and monitor their chart recorder for any sudden drops or peaks that may require them to adjust their trolling depth. The plugs allow the fishermen to present an action-packed bait to the fish as they cover a considerable amount of extra territory than they would normally achieve drifting and deep jigging.

Swimming plugs aren't just confined to the reefs. When fished well offshore, they have proven themselves on dolphin, tuna, and wahoo. In fact, they are a highly popular wahoo bait throughout the Bahamas and Hawaii and are particularly devastating when trolled from a downrigger. By keeping a spinning outfit or two rigged with the plugs, an angler can take advantage of fish that suddenly appear at the surface.

LEADER SELECTIONS

Leader choices for swimming plugs, chuggers, and deep jigs depend on the species. By using the lightest monofilament leader that'll do the job, you'll be increasing a lure's action and ultimately, draw more strikes from fish. A lighter leader also has a thinner diameter that enables it to penetrate the depths quicker than a heavier one. Inshore species, such as small to medium size jacks, trout, bonefish and redfish, can be caught on mono leaders testing 10 or 12 pounds. Snook, tarpon, striped bass, groupers, amberjack and other species with sharp gill plates, or those that inhabit rough terrain, require heavy leaders testing between 40 and 80 pound test. Even some of the toothy species such as mackerel and small barracuda are more likely to strike and be caught on the heavier monofilament leaders rather than wire. However, kingfish and wahoo are two good reasons to switch to wire leaders, even if it's only a trace of about 12 inches.

Using the proper knot is ever so important when fishing jigs, spoons, or plugs. By refraining from drawing a knot snugly against a lure's eye ring, and using primarily an end-loop or uni knot, you'll preserve its actions. With swimming plugs or spoons that are destined for trolling chores, a haywire twist in a wire leader is sufficient. You may even consider running a shock leader between your fishing line and leader. Swimming

Deep jigs probe the water column from the bottom to the top and rate as one of the most effective artificial lures. They can also be cast and retrieved near the surface.

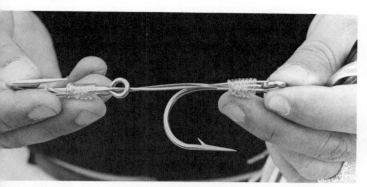

Offshore trollers prefer the stiff rig with hooks offset at 90° for most species. A wire through the eyes of both hooks acts as a stiffener.

When you select an assortment of plugs, make sure that each type will behave differently in the water. That gives you flexibility in presentation.

Small baits frequently fool big fish such as this snook. Light leaders and fine diameter lines impart more realistic action to an artificial lure.

Plugs should be reinspected for damage after each strike. If a lure pulls erratically to one side, slightly bend the eye ring in the opposite direction with a pair of needle nose pliers until the action is corrected. And always inspect hanger-rings for damage, straightening them out as you would the lure's eye ring. Finally, realize that the balsa wood designs, while costing

a bit more, aren't susceptible to taking on water from a puncture wound, typical of big fish and plastic lures.

OFFSHORE LURES

The members in this class make up the true, strictly offshore, trolling lures used to pursue tuna, marlin, and a host of other deep water pelagic species. Comprised of three main divisions, these lures are designed and weighted to troll at speeds faster than those required by natural baits, allowing for more ground coverage during the course of the day. The Kona-Head styles feature a shoveled or cupped head that actually dig through the water. They require the slowest trolling speeds and track in a swimming-like fashion when pulled between eight and 12 knots.

The flat head styles are straight trackers and operate best between 10 and 15 knots. They feature elongated or short heads with blunt faces and come in sizes ranging from a mere five inches for bonito, tuna and dolphin up to those that would make a 500 pound blue marlin think twice about striking them. They're the most versatile lures of the bunch, since they can adapt to and run in just about any sea condition.

The ultra-high speed lures feature a cone or streamlined nose that operates best between 12 and 20 knots. These lures are practical when it comes to covering a vast territory to locate fish and for those anglers who like to troll a lure or two on the way to the fishing grounds. Incidentally, many surprise blue marlin hook-ups have been encountered by anglers leaving or heading for the dock, many miles inside of the reputed hot spots.

For a novice, selecting a set of artificial trolling lures can be confusing. There are sizes, colors, and styles to contend with. The best advice is to select lures that correspond with the fish migrating through the region. For example, if dolphin, tuna, wahoo, sailfish, and white marlin are the primary targets, select artificials in the five through eight inch range. This is a very versatile size that appeals to many species. While blue marlin will readily eat a small lure, other species may not attack, let alone consume, larger baits. If a blue marlin is the goal, stick with the larger lures. Also, make certain the lure and hook sizes aren't over gunning your tackle. You'll need plenty of backbone to drive sizeable hooks home in a fish.

A wide range or flat head lure may be the most practical design. They are effective, and a productive speed is easily obtainable. As far as colors are concerned, fish tend to distinguish only shades rather than specific hues. Dark colors permeate farthest through the water and tend to match the pigmentation of natural baitfish, with red proving to be the least visible color. However, don't get caught up in the colors. The most important factor of any bait or lure is to make it work properly. Once that's accomplished, it's time to look for signs of fish.

Rigging an offshore lure can be as simple as running a monofilament leader through it's eye sleeve and adding a few plastic beads to space the hook and head, or as detailed as creating a stiff rig. One style of rigging the latter involves crimping a hook on one end of a small strip of cable at a 90 degree angle to the thimble or sleeve, crimped on at the opposite end. This trailing hook is usually about five or six inches long. The thimble is then placed over the eye of the lead

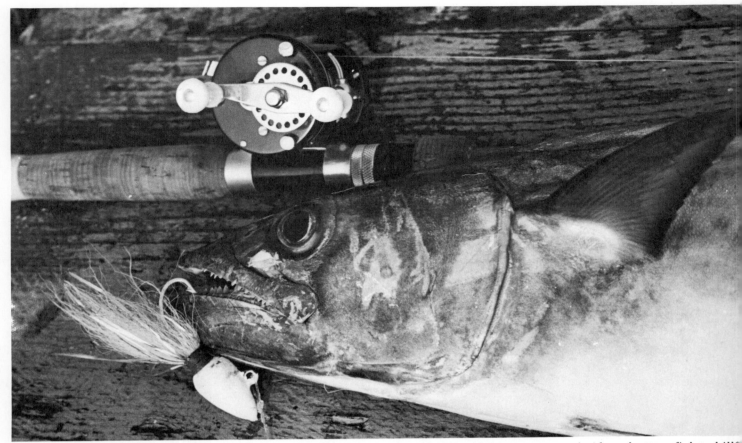

If you had to select a single artificial, it would probably be a leadheaded jig. Almost every species from bottom fish to billfi[sh] will strike it.

hook and held in position with a few wraps of electrical tape. A stainless steel rod is then taped alongside the lead hook and routed through the eye and against the back of the trailing hook. Once it has been bent into shape and trimmed, it is wrapped completely with electrical tape for support. It is now ready to be crimped onto a monofilament leader and placed into action. The key feature behind this rig is its rigidity, which increases the odds of a solid hookup.

Just as the stiff rig has its followers, there are those who believe the free swinging or trailing hook is the ticket. Aside from the manner listed above, hooks can also be snelled to the monofilament. Leader choices usually consist of 15 feet of 300 or 400 pound test monofilament for blue marlin. However, shorter lengths of 100 or 150 pound test monofilament are fine for dolphin, sailfish, white marlin, and tuna. Because of the speeds necessary to operate these lures, wire leader is avoided. The high speed and erratic actions of some lure designs can kink and break a wire leader. Furthermore, by attaching the trailing and lead hook with cable, you'll greatly reduce the threat of cut-offs from wahoo.

High speed lures work best when they're snaking or smoking through the water. Exactly where to place a lure behind the boat will depend on the vessel, speed, and sea conditions. However, make certain the lure occasionally breaks the surface and plows back under, dragging a long trail of aeration in the process. Lures that stay entirely below the surface aren't being pulled fast enough, while those that don't

stay in the brine long enough to form a smoke trail are bei[ng] pulled too quickly. Experimentation is the key. It shouldn't ta[ke] long to develop a feel for lures and learning how to prope[rly] fish them under a variety of sea conditions.

THE IN-BETWEENS

While they can be fished strictly as artificials or in co[n]junction with a natural bait, trolling feathers and weight[ed] skirts are ultra productive offerings that attract the attention [of] almost all marine species. The Jap feather or its modern [o]equivalent consists of a streamlined, chrome-plated lead he[ad] skirted with hackle. It may not look like much in a tackle sh[op] loaded with glamorous lures, but it's in a class by itself whe[n it] comes to producing a variety of fish.

A trolling feather is simply rigged with either wire [or] monofilament leader and a single hook. They come i[n a] variety of sizes and weights and most can be fished adequat[ely] with light tackle. Trolling speeds aren't that critical. Fish th[em] right off the transom or beyond the last bait in the spre[ad.] They'll catch everything from bluefish to tuna.

For years, devoted offshore anglers have used a weigh[ted] skirt or feather in conjunction with a natural bait to hol[d it] below the surface. The sweetened jig's size was increased [as] well, and it became a common target of wahoo and billfi[sh.] While the theory of a weighted skirt remains the same, th[e] facelifts have run the gamut from painted lead to beaut[iful] chrome heads complete with bulging eyes and transluc[ent] skirts. Their productivity or popularity hasn't suffered a bit

CONTROLLED DEPTH FISHING

A top race car driver and a respected fisherman may be worlds apart when it comes to sharing a common interest in their sports, but both are very similar in that they rely on a strategy to win. A race car driver knows that track conditions can change during the course of a show, and the groove that he found so productive during the heat race may not be the quickest way around the track when the main event rolls around. If given ample time, he can adjust his car to compensate against any changes or find the most productive path in action. A wise driver knows how to use the entire track to his advantage, regarding a "single lane" driver as little competition.

Not unlike the race driver, a fisherman realizes that his playing field is constantly changing. He may find superb surface action that seems like it may last forever, only to have it dissipate an hour later. In sharp contrast to the fisherman who only knows how to pursue fish when they're on top, the well seasoned angler will constantly monitor water temperatures and a graph recorder, using various water columns and the thermocline to his advantage.

THE UNDERWATER WORLD

Lowering a bait to fish holding at a specific depth often results in a taker. Given a specific surface temperature of a body of water, it's likely that the readings will decrease significantly toward the bottom. All fish respond to preferred temperatures that dictate their migrations, spawnings, feeding habits and aggressiveness. Fish may be lethargic and unwilling to pursue a lure in a zone of warm water, a few degrees cooler can transform it into a wreckless feeding machine.

Commercial fishermen study thermoclines religiously. With advanced color sonar that displays temperature variations in hues on their screens, they can monitor the zones that appeal to baitfish concentrations. Longliners in pursuit of swordfish make every effort to locate the thermocline. Large concentrations of squid may be just above it. They know that squid is a main staple of broadbills and other species, and that the likelihood of a good haul depends on how accurately their set is made within a productive territory. Where there's bait, there are fish. And that is clearly evident by the longliner's side catch of marlin, sharks, tuna, dolphin, and wahoo.

Inshore and offshore recreational fishermen have been devising ways to get baits down to fish for decades. A sash weight tied to a specified length of nylon cord was often used to lower a bait into the depths. If there was little surface activity, an angler merely tethered out the fishing line, attached it break-away style to the sash weight, and then played out the required amount of line to take it down. It wasn't the slickest of set-ups, but it was a form of controlled depth fishing that resulted in fish that otherwise wouldn't have been caught at the surface. As the concept caught on, the methods of fishing baits below the surface were refined.

Trolling plugs fished relatively deep are becoming increasingly popular with trollers. Plugs are available in several sizes including some over a foot long.

Today, there are several major techniques that are widely practiced.

TROLLING PLANES

Anyone who has spent time aboard a charter boat trolling for kingfish off the Carolina or Texas coasts probably has experienced the effectiveness of a planer. Resembling a modified mousetrap, it is a weighted, stainless steel, diving blade that attains its depth by using water pressure to force it down. The fishing line's swivel is attached to a ring on the planer's support bar. A shock leader, followed by the true leader and bait, is attached to the rear of the unit. When tossed overboard and trolled, the weight and water pressure at the forward portion of the planer will tip it enough so that the eye ring connecting the actual fishing line slides to the rear of its bar. The angle of the blades or wings will resist the water, prompting it to dive deep. A strike from a fish will trip the planer, interrupting the downward force and allowing the eye ring and fishing line to slide forward to change its running angle. Any resistance is eliminated at this point.

The depths attainable by a planer vary with their size and weight, the amount of line played out, and trolling speeds. They can place baits anywhere from a few feet below the surface down to depths nearing 40 feet. Major disadvantages are their near surface level limitations, inability to run at programmed depths, and their drag as they dig through the water. Manually tripping one to check a bait is often a difficult undertaking.

WIRE LINE

Wire or monel line trolling outfits rely on the weight of their solid core fishing lines plus a trolling sinker to pull baits down. Monel wire, an alloy of nickel, copper, iron, manganese, silicon, and carbon, is very resistant to corrosion. Depending on the species sought, anywhere between 30 and 100 yards of monel is attached to a monofilament backing and spooled onto a conventional reel. The rods designed for this style of fishing carry specialized guides that actually channel the line. Roller guides may jam and kink the wire. Terminal tackle also varies, with a small stretch of heavy monofilament shock leader often used to connect the trolling weight and leader.

A bait's depth is primarily regulated by the trolling weight and the amount of line spooled out. As a general rule, for every 100 feet of line, the bait should drop approximately 10 feet deep, with a weight of about 10 ounces and around a five knot trolling speed. Again, precise depth control is questionable. And, like the planer, a wire line outfit is limited mostly to the upper spheres of a water column. In contrast to a planer that trips and offers little resistance when fighting a fish, a wire line outfit is often challenging to retrieve. Aside from the burdensome struggle with the outfit's weight and a stubborn fish, an angler must be careful to lay the monel on the reel smoothly. Any unnecessary "jerking" motions may cause the line to kink. Regardless of its disadvantages (price included), the monel outfit continues to earn its keep aboard many charter and private boats. There are even some captains who believe the hum created by the line dragging through the water is conducive to attracting fish. Recent experiments pitting stainless steel against monel wire have been yielding interesting results.

The cable attains depths comparable with monel, yet doesn't kink as readily and costs less. It may be used with mo[re] regularity in the future.

TROLLING LEADS

Trolling sinkers come in various sizes, shapes, an[d] weights. They are often used in between the actual fishing lin[e] and leader. Eye rings are standard, and most offer eith[er] closed or snap swivels to reduce line twist while trollin[g.] Properly weighted, a trolling bait can be fished at dept[hs] nearing 20 feet. The knack in efficiently using trolling sinke[rs] lies in an angler's ability to determine the zone he wants his ba[it] to ride in and then selecting the lightest lead possible that'll [do] the job. A heavy weight will not only inhibit a bait's action an[d] reduce the hook setting potential, but will place an addition[al] burden on an angler when he is fighting a fish.

The cigar weight and banana sinker are two popul[ar] designs. The cigar lead is weighted evenly and tracks straig[ht] at varying speeds. It is often used in conjunction with trolli[ng] spoons, swimming plugs, and straight tracking baits. As [its] name implies, the banana sinker has a semi-crescent config[u-] ration, with most of its weight distributed throughout its flare[d] bottom or keel. It was originally intended to keep Dacron lin[e] from twisting. Some styles have more of a streamlined appea[r-] ance (compared to the cigar weight), subjecting them to le[ss] resistance when pulled through the water. Others posse[ss] extra wide keels that are designed to use the water to for[ce] them down to greater depths. The disadvantage of trolli[ng] weights, aside from limited depth penetration, is that th[ey] must be watched closely by a person wiring or gaffing a fish [to] avoid a potential injury.

Natural baits, such as mullet and mackerel, can be rigge[d] to swim below the surface by securing an egg sinker und[er] their lower jaws. Again, go with the lightest lead that will gi[ve] them their action and depth. Excess weight within a bait c[an] be a deterrent when they're freespooled to a billfish or [an] equally sensitive fish, and can work to free a hook from [a] jumping fish. A natural bait can also ride below the surface [

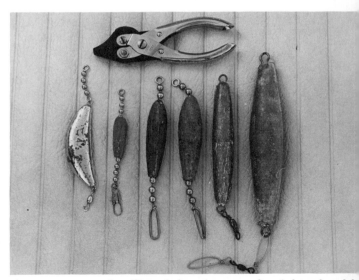

An assortment of trolling sinkers in several weights should [be] aboard every boat. They help to keep an offering just bel[ow] the surface or deeper when necessary.

dding a weighted skirt. Most skirts add appeal to a bait and buffer it against premature washout. Weighted baits are a bit more convenient to use than trolling sinkers, although they'll penetrate only a very limited portion of a water column.

SWIMMING PLUGS

Inshore anglers who troll along channel drop-offs or bridge spans for trout, redfish and other species, know that the length of a swimming plug's lip, combined with the lure's weight, will determine its depth. Most standard plugs operate a foot or two below the surface, while deep divers can penetrate respectable depths. By adjusting a boat's trolling speed and minimizing a fishing line's angle of entry into the water, an angler can pick a spot in the water column.

Swimming plugs fished in relatively shallow waters are effective in covering most depths. However, in deeper systems, it often becomes necessary to go with those that are weighted and have extended lips. These plugs come in various sizes and are capable of attaining depths nearing 20 feet. They are perfect for exploring deep basins, inlet edges, and even offshore reefs. Swimming plugs are versatile lures that should be stored in every angler's tackle box.

DOWNRIGGERS

The evolution of the downrigger marked a major breakthrough in controlled depth fishing. Introduced in fresh water, this versatile unit allows a bait to be effectively fished at practically any zone between the surface and bottom. As the downrigger progressed in design, it ultimately eliminated any confusion over how deep a bait was riding. If a recorder revealed fish 50 feet below the boat, an automatic line counter enabled an angler to lower his bait exactly 50 feet. It proved to be a highly viable tool and the more experienced the angler, the more likely he was to catch fish.

A fabricated downrigger consists of a revolving spool packed with stainless steel cable and a terminal arrangement, a boom (arm) to direct its lead ball away from a boat, and a base that swivels and attaches to a boat's gunwale. Their designs can be simple or complex, with a model for every fishing application. Inshore fishermen can get by with a compact unit that's limited on features and line capacity, while offshore anglers may desire specific features and a spool holding hundreds of feet of cable.

Fishing a downrigger is simple once you've tried it a couple of times. The first step is to establish a normal trolling speed, playing out a bait or lure to a desired position before engaging the reel's drag. Take the fishing line and place it in the release clip that comprises the downrigger's terminal arrangement. After adjusting the tension setting, slowly loosen the downrigger's star-type drag system and simultaneously free spool the reel. Both the bait and downrigger weight (usually 10 pounds) should be lowered slowly to a desired depth, paying particular attention to the line counter. This procedure can be performed single handidly by placing the fishing rod in a holder adjacent to the downrigger. Once the depth is attained, tighten the downrigger's drag only enough to prevent cable slippage, but not to the point where the unit can be damaged by snagging bottom or an underwater obstruction. Engage the fishing reel's drag, taking up the slack until there's a bend in the rod. When a fish strikes, the line will pull free from the clip,

with the rod briefly straightening out before it doubles over again when the line comes tight.

Most downrigger companies offer varying terminal arrangements. The most versatile set up consists of a snap swivel attached at both ends of a three or four inch stretch of 300 pound test monofilament, which the release clip rides on. The lead ball is secured to the bottom snap. The release clip should be sandwiched between a pair of small lead sinkers that'll prevent interference from the crimps securing the monofilament and swivels. The monofilament and swivels eliminate line twist. Quality release clips that offer a precise tension setting are essential. You'll need an ultra light setting to reduce the amount of resistance a fish feels when it takes a live bait and adequate tension to drive the hooks home on the initial strike of a lure or bait that doesn't require a slight dropback. There have been several experiments with various shapes of lead balls and fiberglass depressors in an effort to replace the cumbersome, baseball-like, lead weights. However, they have failed to match the efficiency and effectiveness of the current mainstay.

A downrigger's base should be mounted on a flat surface in the aft section of a boat, where it can be used in conjunction with the gunwale holders. A back-up plate is recommended. A downrigger slides off and on its base easily, making it a breeze to take along on each outing. Most downrigger companies now offer a rod holder insert capped with a flat mounting surface for those anglers who prefer not to drill into a boat's fiberglass to mount a permanent base.

A boom extends a downrigger's cable and lead ball away from the boat. When multiple units are involved, the downriggers closest to the transom often have short bases, while those directly behind them contain longer booms. This arrangement adds space and, similar to outriggers, keeps the baits and weights from interfering with each other. A boom's angle can be locked in a desirable position by tightening the setting at the swivel base. It's imperative that the placement of a downrigger be considered before a boom is selected. There must be enough distance to prevent the cable from touching the prop(s). Furthermore, since most saltwater applications rarely call for more than a pair of downriggers, it may be best to settle for the extra length.

Precise depth control is the main advantage of a downrigger. To maintain a depth indicated on a line counter, an angler must be careful not to exceed a reasonable trolling speed. An increase in speed will cause the cable and weight to plane and lose its accuracy. Should a situation demand a higher trolling speed such as artificial lure fishing, pay out an additional 10 or 20 feet of cable beyond a designated depth. Even with the planing factor, you'll be remarkably close to your mark. Practically any bait can be fished with the aid of a downrigger and an enterprising angler will aim to work all the zones. He'll fish a pair of baits on the surface from the outriggers, one mid depth bait, and the other just above the bottom on a downrigger. If any productive zones exist, he should be able to locate them.

Compared to other forms of controlled depth fishing where permanent weights often become a burden to an angler fighting a fish, a fishing line attached to a downrigger clip pulls free from the unit upon a strike. An angler now has the option of using much lighter tackle than that required by other

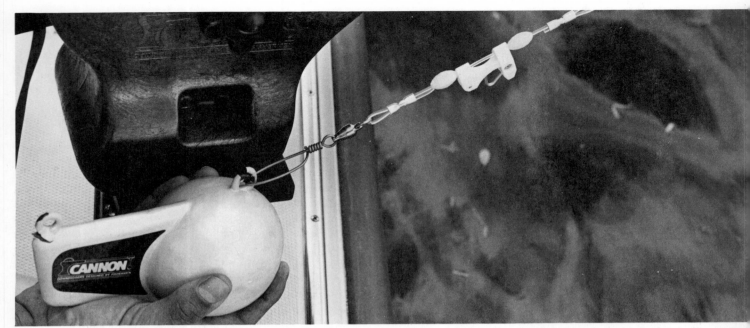

Instead of attaching a downrigger release clip to the back of the weight, you can locate the release above it. A small, outrigg[er] clip on 300-pound mono with a swivel on either end puts the line above the weight.

methods. The only concern should be the need for a free hand in the cockpit to retrieve the lead weight after a strike. Even that's becoming an effortless undertaking, thanks to the introduction of electric downriggers.

Choosing a downrigger that's right for you will depend on your fishing needs and budget. If your fishing is limited mostly to shallow water, selecting a spool that holds several hundred feet of cable is overkill. Likewise, you'll make an expensive mistake by not considering line capacity before purchasing a unit and finding out on the fishing grounds that your new swordfish outfit comes with the entire 50 feet of cable! You should also opt for a line counter that visually displays the amount of cable footage dispatched. Then there's the decision between a manual or electric downrigger, the latter being desired where vast depths must be covered. Today's downrigger has become so sophisticated that there are computerized models that are capable of automatically retrieving the weight after a strike and, once reloaded, lowering it right back to the programmed depth by simply pressing a memory button. They can be programmed to alternate depths throughout the day, and some models even give you a water temperature reading throughout the various zones they visit. All this and more is available to the small boater at fair prices.

DOWNRIGGER VERSATILITY

Fishing versatility is another key feature of a downrigger. They are equally as efficient drift fishing or at anchor as they are trolling. South Florida anglers who used to pursue swordfish when the species population was at a peak drifted an average of three squid baits at varying depths. One bait was fished without a weight and rode at or near the surface. Another bait had break away weights (sinkers attached lightly to the fishing line with copper wire) and was fished between 50 and 100 feet deep, while a third weighted outfit rested closer to 200 feet. Those who relied on downriggers were relieved of the headaches and extra work of tethering lines

and trying to approximate their depths. They simply attach[ed] the line to the release clip and lowered the bait. Checking [or] replacing a bait was accomplished within minutes.

Tuna fishermen who either drift or anchor and chunk f[or] fish are discovering how convenient downriggers are in sta[g]gering baits at various depths. Gone are the headaches [of] measuring line, tying balloons, and securing sinkers, hopi[ng] that they break away on a strike. And a downrigger needn't [be] limited to offshore applications. They're very effective ov[er] shallow reefs for migrating fish, such as kingfish, mackerel [and] bluefish, and really produce for those fishermen trolling swi[m]ming plugs or baits near the bottom for grouper, snapper [and] sea bass. Even the casual angler who anchors up on a reef [or] wreck and chums for yellowtails can place a whole bait rig[ht] off the bottom for a large grouper, jewfish, amberjack a[nd] snapper and not interfere with his regular game of freelini[ng] baits with the current.

Downriggers are effective in lowering live bait to sailfi[sh] when they refuse to come to the top, and are quite viable [in] tight confines such as fishing near a wreck or bridge piling[s.] Fishermen can either anchor or hold a boat in position [in] current of a wreck and drift a bait just inches above t[he] structure without the threat of a snag. Tarpon migrate annual[ly] throughout the Florida Keys and often linger around bridge[s.] Anglers generally will anchor up current of a bridge, letti[ng] out enough scope so that they can drift their baits back und[er] the span. With a downrigger, not only can the baits be fished [at] or near the surface, but right on the bottom where tarpon [do] most of their feeding. And an angler won't have to worry abo[ut] any cumbersome weights after the strike.

There are really no limitations on a downrigger. It pr[o]vides the best and most effective depth penetration and c[an] be used efficiently both inshore and offshore. By experimen[t]ing with a unit, you'll be able to come up with some of yo[ur] own applications. In the long run, your experience with [a] downrigger will be reflected in your catch.

BOTTOM BOUNCING

Searching for fish along the floors of oceans, bays and sounds ranks as the most popular form of salt water fishing, and for good reason. Bottom fishing usually offers plenty of action, which can range from rigging gear and baiting hooks to judging when to set up on a pernicious fish that's been nibbling away at an offering. In contrast to trolling or other specialized forms of fishing, there's always something to keep an angler's mind occupied, and the odds are greater for finding more consistent fishing. Furthermore, most benthic fish provide good to excellent tablefare.

LOCATING STRUCTURE

The concept behind successful bottom fishing is based on an angler's ability to uncover structure that is likely to hold fish. Structure can be defined as wrecks, reefs, rockpiles, depressions in the bottom's contour, weed growth, bridges and assorted rubble, pilings and even channel edges. Anything that offers sanctuary is likely to be an ecosystem that harbors both bait and gamefish. As algae and micro organisms begin to flourish on or near such points, smaller fish move in to feed and seek shelter and, in turn, attract larger fish. Depending upon the size and location of the structure, a complete community is often maintained, with the larger benthic fish establishing their own niches within the boundaries. If such territorial fish are removed from the system, there will be others that'll quickly replace them.

Regardless of size, fish spell happiness. There are countless opportunities for fun from docks, seawalls, and the shoreline.

Expert anglers realize how critical structure is to success. It's not unusual for them to run long and hard before settling down to fish, with the excessive travel time often rewarded with quality catches. Probably the most valuable aid when it comes to bottom fishing is a dependable chart recorder. Used by all professional captains and an ever increasing number of recreational anglers, a recorder offers the advantages of illustrating an entire water column. It shows whether a bottom's composition is hard (rocky) or soft (muddy), the exact zone in which the fish are holding and, to some degree, it differentiates between bait and gamefish.

When ferreting out productive structures in an unfamiliar region, anglers should first study a navigational chart. By doing this homework, which includes chatting with local baitshop personnel, one can pencil in and then locate several proven areas. The chart recorder helps to pinpoint the exact spot by monitoring the bottom's contour. Furthermore, anglers often run to such spots with their recorders on. They may burn excessive amounts of paper in the process, but there's always the possibility of uncovering fish and new structures along the way.

Loran has greatly simplified the ability to find and return to a hot area. In addition, the coordinates of the more popular points are often public knowledge, reducing the amount of effort and headaches associated with trying to locate them by other means. A professional captain will always study a chart recorder for structure, placing the loran coordinates of promising areas into the unit's memory. Over the years, these captains have logged hundreds of spots in the pages of their loran books. By taking the time to record their findings, they have literally created a fishing circuit. A captain now has the option of lining up several prominent spots within striking distance of each other. If one point fails to produce fish, he'll simply plug in another set of coordinates and continue on his way. It may take a few years to master, but recreational anglers can build their own collection of numbers, as well as determine what spots are best during the course of a year.

DIFFERENT STROKES FOR DIFFERENT FOLKS

By developing a basic understanding of the most popular fish frequenting a region, you should have an advantage that will reflect in your catch. Focus on the seasons, the types of structure that appeal to them, the best baits, and coordinating your terminal gear with the size and species of the fish.

For example, blackfish is a very popular northeastern groundfish that takes up residence around scattered rocks in sounds and shallow offshore waters, becoming more abundant between spring and fall. These scrappy warriors, often less than four pounds, lurk around structure for protection and to feed on various types of mussels and clams. Anglers fishing Long Island Sound off Rowayton, Connecticut, particularly around Green's Ledge, Budd Reef and The Cows off Shippan Point (just north of the Stamford breakwater), benefit from abundant rockpiles that maintain healthy populations of these tasty fish.

Black seabass are similar to blackfish except that they prefer slightly greater depths and are more prominent offshore of the Carolina and Virginia coastlines. From the Carolinas southward through the Gulf of Mexico, groupers and snappers take over as the most valuable bottom fish.

WRECK DWELLERS

Artificial reefs and shipwrecks have improved local fisheries by replacing portions of the bottom that have been damaged, and by adding structure to otherwise barren areas. Most wrecks and artificial reefs are situated offshore, although an increasing amount of attention is being given to developing inshore programs. Species visiting or taking up residence around these points run the gamut from amberjack, barracuda, cobia (ling), snapper, and grouper from the Gulf of Mexico to the Carolinas. Cod, pollack and hake take over in the cooler waters off the New England coast.

Seasons will determine the arrival of migratory species. Peaks can range from the winter in the extreme southern portion of Florida to the spring and early summer off the southeast and Gulf of Mexico states to mid summer and early fall off the northeast. Because of the vast ecosystems supported by these wrecks, pelagic species sometimes linger around the ones situated near deep water. Dolphin, kingfish and mackerel may visit sights in the Gulf of Mexico and southeastern states, and every now and again there might be a smattering of sailfish and tarpon off some of the South Florida wrecks.

DEEP DWELLERS

The ultra deep species that reside on the bottom near and beyond the Continental Shelf make up a small recreational fishery due to the vast depths and currents that must be encountered to get a bait down to them. Tilefish are probably the most popular and abundant species, followed by hake and cusk in the northeast. Since it's sometimes necessary to make a set at depths nearing 2,000 feet, especially for the latter two species, electric reels are used to lower and haul up the heavily weighted rigs. You will occasionally find recreational anglers fishing for tilefish in waters around 400 feet deep with electric reels or downriggers that have enough cable to reach them.

INSHORE FISH

Inshore species are located in a manner similar to their offshore counterparts, but their structure will consist of scattered debris, channel edges, depressions, oyster bars, etc. The prestigious striped bass is a prime example of an inshore species that frequents shelves and rocky points. It is especially fond of structure at the mouths of rivers or canals that dump fresh and brackish waters into bays and sounds. Compared to blackfish which can sometimes be found around offshore rocks, striped bass rarely travel seaward.

Gulf coast and southeastern bay anglers know that the popular sheepshead can be found around hard bottom. Alabama's Mobile Bay is just one productive system that yields great numbers of these fish. The remains of the old Dauphin Island bridge and the surrounding oyster beds attract some real heavyweights that may break five or six pounds. The tasty fish feed mainly on crustaceans that abound around such structure.

Species such as flounder or fluke (summer flounder) are fond of structure, too. However, in comparison to hard bottom, these fish enjoy muddy bottoms that are adjacent shallow flats, as well as various holes, depressions or channel Their flat configuration and coloration permit them to blen into the ocean floor. This camouflage offers both protectio and the ability to attack unsuspecting baitfish such as bloo and sand worms, mussels, killiefish and sand eels. The flu grows considerably larger than the winter flounder, with doc mats weighing more than ten pounds. It'll frequent sections inlets and shoals where moderate to swift currents abound

THE FUN FISH SPECIES

If the most sought after species take a breather, there ar always the "fun fish" that will do their best to turn an otherwis unproductive day into a memorable outing. Some of thes lesser known fish aren't recommended for quality tablefar but practically all of them will put up a determined scrap wit anglers who are willing to scale their tackle accordingly. Da savers can include pinfish, which are caught over grassy fla in the Gulf and Southeastern coastal states, porgies (scup white perch, grunts, sea robins, blowfish, etc. All species ar prominent inshore and over some offshore structures and ar usually under two pounds. Their willingness to consume variety of small cut baits make them the perfect challenge fo youngsters who are just beginning to experience the thrill c salt water angling.

GETTING TO THE FISH

Although some inshore fish, such as flounder, stripe bass, porgies, and blackfish, can be taken by anglers fror bridges, piers or in the surf, increased fishing pressure ha limited the better catches to boat owners. After locating potential area, an angler must select the baits and use them i conjunction with the proper rigs to get them down to the fish Always obtain the freshest bait possible. Bottom fish, partic ularly grouper and snapper, rely heavily on their sense of sme and it often takes the scent of a fresh bait to convince a finick member to eat. While you may take your fair share of fish o frozen bait, there's no denying that a fresh bait will be th decisive factor in producing fish on slow days.

An experienced bait fisherman always takes into consic eration what's happening around him. That is, he's monitorin the water conditions to find out what the fish are feeding o and using the bait that's the most abundant within an area. B "matching the hatch", an angler can increase his chances c catching fish. There are many species that go on a selectiv feeding pattern, consuming those baits that they hav rounded up or which thrive in a system. Striped bass is just on species that tends to specialize at times. Veteran anglers kno they'll score more consistently by using the predominant bai

Understand that fish frequenting grass flats or soft bo toms are often pursuing shrimp, crabs or bloodworms an those over rockpiles are ferreting out crabs, mussels and variety of baitfish. Try tempting the fish with their natural foo first, switching strategies only after there's a lull in the activit Furthermore, it often requires alternating baits when fis become wise to a certain offering. For example, groupe fished over the rockpiles in the Gulf of Mexico are noted fo turning off to a specific type of bait that's repeatedly lowere into their domain. That's why successful anglers begin b using only one type of offering, such as Spanish sardines, an witching to another, usually squid, mullet or live pinfish, when the fish cease feeding. By doing so, they can effectively take advantage of a concentration of fish.

Neatness counts in trimming baits. There's more to presenting natural baits than cutting a chunk from a fish and lowering it to the bottom. Consider the current and how much more enticing a strip of squid or mullet will be if it flutters in front of a fish's lair. Baits can be trimmed to create a swimming action, and even to conceal a hook, such as a ballyhoo plug. A streamlined bait will cut accurately through a swift tide, appealing more to fish than a bulky one that resists the flow. Above all, pack several different types of baits on each outing. You'll not only have a greater chance of supplying the fish with what they want, but have an adequate back-up supply that can even be used for chum.

Fresh baits and proper terminal tackle make a difference in bottom fishing. Rods should have enough backbone to pump one's quarry to the top.

TERMINAL GEAR

Successful bottom fishing requires a precise balance of terminal gear tailored to the desired species. Many fishermen make the mistake of employing gear that is too heavy for their quarry. Such overkill results in fewer strikes, affects a bait or lure's action, and reduces the sensitivity to feel a fish pick up an offering. Whenever applicable, use the lightest monofilament leaders that can handle a species and the least amount of lead

that will hold an offering at the bottom. Depending upon the structure and the size of the fish, you may even consider scaling down to light tackle, such as 10 or 12 pound test line. The smaller diameter of a light line allows it to sink quicker than a heavier one and increases its sensitivity. Also, the lighter the monofilament leader, the less hardware a fish is likely to notice.

There will be certain situations that will prohibit the use of light gear. When fishing near wrecks or abrupt structures for large fish such as grouper or snapper, it's often necessary to employ heavy gear to horse the fish away from a potential cutoff. However, by utilizing a monofilament leader that tests slightly above the actual fishing line, you can still benefit by keeping visibility minimal. If an angler is fishing a wreck for grouper averaging 15 or 20 pounds and uses 30 pound test line, his leader's breaking strength should be 40 or 50 pounds. If he uses a 20 pound test outfit, he should reduce his leaders to around 30 or 40 pound test. Grouper don't possess dentures that are detrimental to fishing lines and it's often beneficial to use light to moderate strength leaders for them. Even with toothy fish such as mackerel or kingfish, you'll draw more strikes by using predominantly monofilament leaders. To reduce the risk of a cut-off and still maintain low visibility, tie a three or four inch wire trace leader to the monofilament with an Albright Special knot.

Sinkers come in a variety of sizes and shapes to cover most bottom applications. Among the standard selections that attach directly to the fishing line are the split shots (a small lead that is crimped on a fishing line) and the rubbercore sinker (which is attached by running the fishing line through its groove with a rubber cap or stop at each end to hold it in place). The egg sinker is the common choice of bottom fishermen. If the lead is small enough, it can ride just above the eye of a hook. Otherwise, most applications will find it resting on a swivel or the knot joining the fishing line and leader.

The pyramid sinker is often used in swift currents. In contrast to the weight styles mentioned above, the pyramid actually anchors itself in the bottom, leaving the bait to ride freely just above it. Like the egg sinker, the pyramid can be rigged as a slider by running the fishing line through its eye. It also can be used as a base for specialty rigs where two or more hooks are featured.

The type of terminal arrangement an angler chooses will depend on the species and his sporting virtues. For example, a rig for striped bass can consist of an egg sinker just above a three or four foot stretch of 60 pound test monofilament leader and a 6/0 or 7/0 live bait hook. The bait can be a live menhaden, or the head section of one. Rigs for blackfish, grouper and seabass can be as simple as a 2/0 hook, a foot or so of 30 or 40 pound test monofilament leader, and an adequate amount of lead to maintain a proper depth. A more complex dropper rig would incorporate a pyramid sinker at its base and about three or four feet of 60 pound test monofilament leader equally divided by a pair of three-way swivels, each featuring about a two foot dropper line with a hook.

There are anglers who are fond of a spreader rig, particularly with flounder. Such an instrument is constructed with a three way swivel dividing 20 — 24 inches of stiff wire. The fishing line is tied to the swivel's top eye with a few inches of monofilament and a bank or pyramid sinker attached to the bottom. A dropper hook is then secured to each end of the wire bar.

Regardless of the rigs, hook sizes should be geared to the species of fish. A large hook shows more hardware and requires a serious effort to drive it home, especially with species blessed with bony jaws. Take the time to hone each hook before placing it into action, inspecting it for sharpness throughout the day.

DEEP JIGGING

Deep jigging involves the art of coaxing a fish to strike an artificial. It's a popular form of fishing that is often associated with light tackle. The advantage of deep jigging is that you work not only the ocean bottom, but the entire water column. Grouper anglers in South Florida, The Bahamas, and the Keys continually see action from pelagic species such as kingfish, mackerel, barracuda and even a sailfish over the deep, offshore reefs. In addition, the boat usually drifts along a reef, allowing an angler to cover more ground and increase his chances of finding fish.

Deep jigs come in a variety of sizes and shapes. The two most prominent designs include the lima bean and arrow heads. The lima bean style features compressed sides that give it a fluttering action when worked through the water. The arrow tends to track straight and accurately. The latter design also penetrates a water column quicker because it exposes less surface area. Jigging spoons are more prominent in northern waters. Like the lead heads, they, too, come in various weights and two main designs that give them an inherent action. The diamond jig slices through the water quickly, while those featuring flat sides maintain a swimming like motion.

To maximize a jig's action and potential, use the lightest weight possible to reach bottom. Depending upon the species, opt for the lightest monofilament leader that can accomplish the job. If you have to use wire to prevent a cut-off, try a trace of about four or five inches. Pay particular attention to the knot, making sure there's an adequate loop for the jig to swing on. Ditto with wire. Never snug a knot against a lead's eye ring, for it will only hinder its performance.

A productive drift pattern is one that covers the shallow and deep sections of a reef. Depending upon the wind and tide, begin your drift at one extreme, repositioning yourself only after you clear the opposite end. By covering various depths and working closely with a chart recorder, you'll be able to discover the most productive zones to concentrate on. For benthic species, a jig should be allowed to reach bottom before being retrieved back to the surface with a hopping motion. It often pays to let the jig sink back to the bottom a second time after initially retrieving it about 20 feet. A solid strike will get an angler's attention in a hurry. Fish often strike a jig on its descent, reducing an angler's ability to "feel" the fish. If there's the slightest interference with a jig destined for the bottom, engage the reel's drag, take up the slack line, and strike if there's any resistance.

Often frowned upon by purists, sweetening a jig with a natural bait is almost a sure fire way of luring bottom dwellers into feeding. Sweeteners can include strips of cut bait trimmed

Deep jigs come in a variety of head shapes. Each one has different action in the water. Many anglers increase th appeal by hanging a plastic worm from the hook.

so that they flutter attractively with the jig's motion, or who baits that are impaled on a hook. Tipped jigs can be retrieve in a fashion listed above or left on the bottom until a fis consumes it. A second hook can even be added to guar against short strikes. Trailing hooks feature open eyes that ca be closed with pliers after they've been attached to the lea hook. The lead hook is inserted under the bait's lower jaw ar out the upper membrane with the barb of the second hoc positioned inside the mid section.

CHUMMING

Chumming and bottom fishing often go hand in han Chumming helps attract and gather fish from various struc tures and motivates them to feed. Because of the keen comp tition, fish are more likely to attack a bait when they are in pack or school.

Effectively chumming a reef or structure requires a bo to be anchored upcurrent from the target point. That way, tl scent and morsels drift into the crevices and lure both bait ar gamefish into the open. A regulated dispersal rate will kee enough chum flowing for the fish to follow its trail, where the will eventually come upon the loaded baits. Too much chu and the fish will be content to lie in their lairs and feed un their needs are satisfied.

Gulf of Mexico anglers searching for grouper and sna per chum into rockpiles with either shrimp boat by-produc or sections of Spanish sardines. They'll place a fresh bait or lightweight bucktail and let the offering rest on the botto When the fish venture from their structures, they'll have lit problem locating the bait. Chum bases vary with regions. Th can range from frozen blocks of ground fish, which thaw a regulated pace from within a mesh bag floating off the tra som, to cat and dog food, segments of bait, and discarded fi and crabs from shrimpers.

A mild current which spreads the chum throughout t target area is ideal. When currents become too swift, the chu is quickly carried away at the surface and can't drift down where it'll be effective. There are a variety of remedies compensate for such conditions. Mixing sand with chum a dispatching the concoction in balls adds weight to carry t food down before it disperses. You can attach four or fi

atural baits, such as Spanish sardines, to a heavy jig and work
hem free at the bottom. Try stashing weights in a chum bag or
owering the chum on a downrigger. However, the last two
echniques should require the chum bag to be tied "breaka-
ay" style in case of shark attacks.

PARTY BOATS

Party or drift boats provide access to bottom fish and are
n inexpensive alternative to chartering a private craft. They
ffer a great day on the water with friends when you don't feel
ke going through the motions of preparing your own craft.
rices on these boats vary, but you can expect to pay an
verage of $12 to $25 dollars per person for a half or full day
cket respectively. The fishing strategies will also vary with
hat's running at the time. If migratory species are in, expect
e drift and tackle to be geared towards them. Although you
an still drop a bait to the bottom, the odds are that the boat
on't be positioned over prime ground fish spots.

Check with a party boat captain in advance to learn
hat's running, his strategy for the week, prices, and the type
f gear he has available. Chances are reservations aren't
quired and, unless you prefer your own gear, tackle is usually
vailable at a nominal rental fee. Ditto terminal gear. Also, find
ut what baits he'll have on board, packing your own if you
elieve a different offering may stack the deck in your favor.
arty boats make their money on the number of fishermen
ey host. Therefore, heavy tackle (30 and 40 pound test
onventional gear), is the norm. If you plan on bringing light
ckle, it may be best to consult the captain in advance. If the
ail" is lean, he may let you follow through with your quest.
therwise, a disaster is almost sure to occur if a fish hooked on
ght tackle skirts its way across and tangles the lines of about
) other paying customers.

Productive positions or hot seats aboard a party boat are
ose which happen to be near the fish when they're passing
rough, or right above an edge, shelf, wreck or structure.
any anglers swear by the stern, although their preference
ay be based on the fact that they're not sandwiched between
her anglers, and that their baits can be drifted or worked in
e relatively uncrowded waters off that section. If you desire a

*arty boats specialize in different species. Be sure to select a
oat that will fish for the species you want to catch.*

stern slot, make certain you arrive at the dock well ahead of
time to secure it. And by all means, make sure you board the
craft at least 15 minutes before departure. Party boat captains
adhere precisely to their designated schedule to maximize
actual fishing time.

The backbone of any drift boat is the mate. This hard
working lad must cater to the needs of the ship's party. He's in
charge of rigging tackle, baiting hooks, untangling lines, keeping anglers happy, cleaning fish for anglers, and keeping the
boat and its gear in ship shape and Bristol fashion. He's only
too happy to explain the most productive techniques for the
designated species, simply looking for a little consideration in
the form of a tip back at the dock.

Party boat techniques are as simple as using a strip of bait
or a whole fish on a hook and sending it down with the aid of a
weight. The idea is to keep the bait just above the bottom,
which is usually accomplished by taking a few turns on a reel
after it reaches its destination. Periodically, drop the bait back
down to the bottom to compensate for any line planing due to
current. After several minutes, it becomes necessary to reel
up, check the bait, and re-drop it to keep an advantageous
angle with the bottom. Deep jigging techniques also will
produce, although it can become very difficult to entice a fish
to strike an artificial when there's plenty of natural bait to be
had. Some drift boat captains will go so far as to deploy a live
bait or two in hopes of capturing a shark, billfish or other
trophy fish for mounting purposes. If you desire to fish a live
bait, make arrangements with the captain at least a day or so in
advance.

Some drift boats even offer weekend bottom fishing
expeditions to remote regions at very attractive rates, especially those sailing from South Florida and the Keys. Drift boats
operate half and full day trips, as well as some night outings.

FIGHTING STRATEGIES

Bottom fish can be pursued with almost any type of gear.
The smaller members frequenting grass beds, oyster bars,
bridges, etc., are enjoyable to wrestle on lines testing less than
ten pound test. The bigger gladiators are a different story.
Depending on an angler's skill, he may attempt to challenge
some of these critters on bait-casting gear spooled with lines
testing between 12 and 15 pounds. However, when large fish
abound over potentially dangerous structures, it often
requires stiff rods and a minimum of 20 pound test line to have
a chance at them.

The strategy with bottom fish, even with the smaller
species on ultra light gear, is to go toe-to-toe with them
immediately after setting the hook. By placing as much strain
on your tackle as you can and still keeping within the line's
breaking strength, you'll have a better chance of disorienting
the fish enough to move it away from any structure. Any delays
will give the fish a fighting chance, and usually enough time to
react and charge into its lair. If a fish holes up, try throwing
slack in the line for a few minutes, then engaging the reel's
drag and "horsing" the fish after the line becomes taut. There
are no guarantees, but sometimes this trick is worthy of a try.
The most critical stage of the battle usually ends about ten or
15 feet above the bottom. It's a game of reflexes and judgement that becomes mastered after a few seasons in the field.

BASIC SINKERS

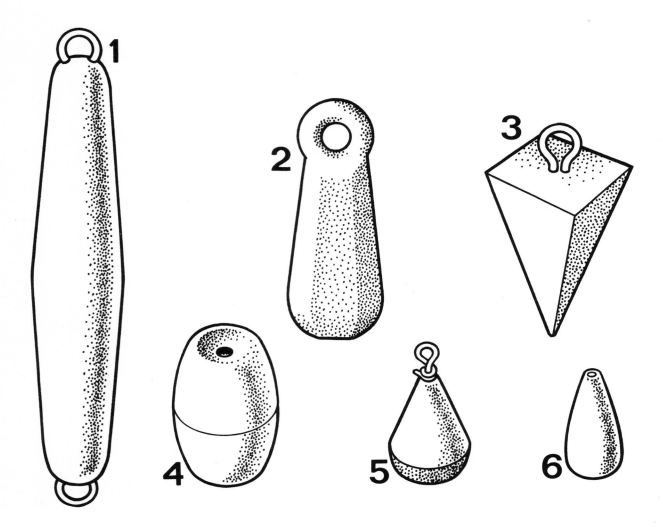

Choosing the right sinker for a specific task contributes significantly to angling success. Each shape of the hundreds available has been designed to perform best under certain conditions. Match the sinker to the type of fishing you plan to do and you should catch more fish. Regardless of sinker shape, always use the lightest weight that will do the job.

The Torpedo (1) is tailored for trolling assignments. There are variations that incorporate bead chain and snaps on the end. It can also be used to get a heavy bait down to mid-depth or the bottom. Experts insist that the Bank (2) represents the most efficient sinker design. It casts well, drops to the bottom quickly, and is targeted toward broken and rocky terrain or reefs.

Pyramids (3) also have wide appeal and work best on relatively soft and smooth bottoms. The edges tend to dig in and anchor the sinker. Surf fishermen and those who fish over unstructured turf rely on the pyramid. With a hole through the center, the Egg (4) is an in-line sinker that is very popular throughout the southern states. It works as a fish-finder, allowing the line to be pulled while the sinker remains stationary.

The Dipsey (5) rolls around the bottom in a current and does a nice job when you want the bait to move slowly with tide or current. Bullet weights (6) have a number of marine uses. Rigged with a plastic tail, they enable the caster to incorporate a variety of retrieves from swimming at mid-depth to hopping across the bottom. They can be used to form daisy chains of trolling lures or to add weight to a feather.

THE FLATS

Shallow water forms a unique and demanding habitat where exceptionally wary gamefish abandon the sanctuary. and safety of the depths to search for food. It is a marginal zone that lures the angler to an unparalleled and unforgiving challenge in which he stalks his quarry more as a hunter than a fisherman. A mistake is costly; victory is well-earned.

Striped bass invade the flats of San Francisco Bay when the tide is inviting. Three thousand miles eastward, jumbo bluefish charge across the skinny portions of Chesapeake Bay each spring because the menhaden are there. Along the Texas Coast, the redfish tails as it ferrets out a morsel from the countless miles of estuary. Down in Florida, bonefish, permit, tarpon, sharks, barracuda, jacks, mutton snapper, and other critters venture in water that barely covers their backs simply because they are hungry.

Timing is everything. There are primary seasons, critical water temperatures, and specific stages of the tide with which to contend. The fish aren't there around the clock or the calendar. Selecting the correct conditions becomes part of the game. Even veteran guides may be fooled more often than they are willing to admit. It's a search operation where silence and stealth count, because a fish out of its element becomes nervous and skittish, ready to bolt at the first inkling of a problem. That holds true for oversized sharks with rows of dentures as well as the wily bonefish or stubborn redfish.

In the southeastern corner of Florida and throughout the Caribbean, most flats are as clear as the liquid in a bottle of spring water. Along the Gulf Coast and in San Francisco Bay, the shallows are much more turbid, a condition that persists the farther north one travels. Even on murky flats, it is possible to see fish or signs of fish.

BE PREPARED

Without polarized sunglasses and a broad-brimmed hat to build a tent around your eyes, there is no meaningful vision on the flats. Skippers tell story after story about people with expensive sunglasses who cannot spot fish simply because those glasses do not have polarized lenses. Nothing else cuts through the surface glare.

The hat's brim should have a dark underside that absorbs light rather than reflects it. Wrap around glasses or side shields also help to keep extraneous light from getting to the eyes. On tropical flats with white, puffy clouds overhead, the brightness can be taxing on the eyes. Always carry a spare pair of polarized glasses and an extra hat for emergencies. Browns and tans work better on the flats than the green, gray, or bluish tints. Some anglers also buy a pair of polarized glasses in a lighter shade for overcast days, early morning, and late afternoon.

Necessity forces any fish hooked in shallow water to put up a horizontal battle rather than a vertical one. When you lean back on the rod, you can expect that critter on the other end to streak for the drop off and deeper water. Long, fast runs dictate reels with smooth drags and adequate line capacities.

If you are going to fish the flats, make certain your tackle is up to the task. Rods should have tips tailored to cast the

talking fish on the shallow flats demands silence and concentration. One casts only when the fish is seen. Speed and accuracy of presentation are essential ingredients. Polarized sunglasses and a broad-brimmed hat are musts.

necessary weight bait or lure and enough backbone or reserve power to withstand the stubborn brawl that will surely result. A single casting outfit is seldom enough. Rig at least two or three combinations with different offerings on the end. For bluefish, you might have a surface chugger, darter, and a leadhead. Those San Francisco stripers respond to rattling plugs, topwater, and a variety of jigs. Changing baits on the same rod wastes time and there is a tendency to stick with what you are using. It's much easier to pick up another outfit, make a few casts, and then go back to what you were using.

The tropics boast a greater variety of fish on the flats, offering the option of opportunity fishing. Specialists may set their sights on bonefish, tarpon, or permit, but it's fun and rewarding to be ready for sharks, barracuda, and anything else that happens along. If you have several rods rigged in advance, you can switch over by picking up the right outfit which has been carefully laid out at your feet.

Flats fishing focuses on casting and one can use spinning, bait casting, or fly tackle in the quest. There are a few situations where it is possible to fish live or dead natural bait while anchored or staked out. Whatever method or methods you choose, check the tackle carefully and be sure it operates perfectly. Nothing is more frustrating than to make a cast right on target and then lose the fish because a worn line failed or the reel had an erratic drag that finally failed to yield.

GO WITH THE FLOW

Tides are critical in shallow water. Acres of real estate may be void of any visible life on one stage of the tide and a veritable fish bowl on another. The key to success lies in knowing when to be at a particular spot. Interestingly, there are places that produce fish on incoming tide and other locations a long cast away that only have life on outgoing water. If you are fishing unfamiliar waters without a local guide, the basic rule is to start on the first of the incoming tide and follow the flow of water higher on the flat. Fish generally move inshore on rising water and drop off toward deeper terrain as the tide falls.

Spring tides occur around the period of the new and full moons, bringing a greater range and a stronger push of water. Neap tides take place around the quarter moons. Generally, flats fishing is better on the spring tides, but there are places where too much water scatters the fish and they are difficult to locate. Experience and local knowledge help to solve these problems.

From a safety standpoint, you should be alert to the stage of the tide. On some flats, this can be tricky. There are places where the water empties as quickly as if you pulled the plug on a bathtub. It's easy to get stranded by receding water and have to wait six hours or more before you get off the shallows. That's not much fun in a skiff, particularly when darkness is approaching. Sharks often serve as a good indicator of water depth. If you see them dropping off a flat, it may be time for you to go with them.

THE APPROACH

Outboard engine noise scares fish, particularly in water barely deep enough to cover their backs. If you persist in running over shallow water at flank speed, fishing on those flats could be disappointing. Those fish that didn't flee for a

distant sanctuary become skittish and even uncooperative. There are times when your quarry won't be too badly shake by the sudden noise, but veteran anglers prefer the siler approach.

Based on the species, its habits, and the tide stage, yo should pick a starting point before you get near the fla. Throttle down while still in deep water and putt-putt to th edge. Use a pushpole to propel and guide the boat. In murk waters where blind casting becomes the rule rather than th exception, locals often drift the flats while fanning their cas to cover as much water as possible. On the first drift, idle i well above the area you plan to fish and let wind and currer carry you quietly through the productive zone. Then, moto out very slowly and run back in deep water to repeat the drift o to work another part of the flat. Stay away from territory yo intend to fish.

Poling a boat borders on hard work, but it brings results. you are fishing the first of the incoming tide, you'll have to wo back and forth along the edge, moving higher as the wate floods. Species such as bonefish, permit, and redfish tend swim into the tide, because they use their sense of smell help them find food. By working back and forth across th tide, you have a better chance of finding the fish.

Keep in mind that water depth can be critical. A fe inches sometimes spell a major difference in where fish will and where they won't. It's possible to overrun the fish whi easing inshore on a rising tide. If you don't see anything, dro back a bit and take another look. Follow a zigzag pattern un you locate your quarry. Then, you can concentrate on th depth. Remember, however, that things change as the tic continues to flood or fall.

Life for the poler becomes much easier when wind o tide and the sun is at his back. You want the sun behind you aid vision and make it more difficult for the fish to see yo Going with the wind or tide (whichever is stronger), makes li more tolerable and also enables you to cast with or across th wind rather than into it.

Poling should be done at a leisurely pace, giving all hanc more time to search for fish. It's amazing how a school can sl by or denizens weighing more than 100 pounds ghost without detection. There are spots that lend themselves staking the boat and waiting for the fish to come to yo Picking the right location demands local knowledge. At som

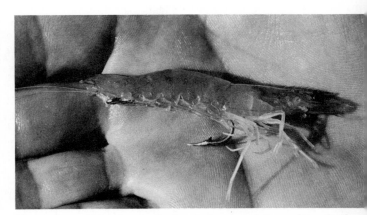

By cutting off the fan tail of a shrimp and threading the hoo through the body, it will cast farther and more accurately.

Unless you have experience and local knowledge, it's important to fish the flats with a guide first. He'll put you in the right area and help you spot the fish.

places, the boat must be repositioned as the water level rises or falls. If you are not in the critical spot, you won't see fish.

THE SEARCH

Looking is one thing; seeing is quite another. To spot fish on a flat or detect signs of your quarry's presence, you must concentrate. It's a mental discipline as well as a physical one. If you fish the off-color flats, scout the surface for clues to any form of activity. It could be a swirl or a boil or the sight of water being pushed by a school of fish. Scan great distances frequently. You may see some activity a quarter mile away or more. As you work the lure, use those polarized glasses to see beneath the surface or right behind the lure. Surprisingly, you should be able to pick out any fish that follows the artificial. Don't overlook slicks, muds, or anything else out of the ordinary.

When the water is reasonably shallow and a fish noses downward to root on the bottom, its tail lifts above the surface and waves in the air. Fish have a tendency to tail early and late in the day and especially when the water is relatively calm. If you are looking out across the surface, you should be able to spot the silvery tail of a bonefish, the bronze caudal fin of the redfish, or the sickle-shape of the permit. The tails may only wave for an instant or two, but the alert angler has them pinpointed.

The higher you are above the water, the easier it is to see into it. Along the Gulf Coast, scooters and other boats have tall towers. Skiff users put platforms over the engine to gain elevation. Anglers in the bow sometimes stand atop coolers to gain an edge. In the tradeoff, the higher one stands, the easier it is for the fish to spot him.

When the water is murky, you may not see the whole fish. It's somewhat akin to spotting a deer in the woods. You may not see the entire shape, but you should still be able to identify the animal. Redfish in Gulf waters are difficult to see at times, but with concentration, it's possible. Only part of the red may

be visible, but that's the clue for which you've been searching.

It takes practice to see fish. The trick centers on staring through the surface of the water as if it were a pane of glass. Focus on the bottom or just above it. Your eyes should scan the area as if they were a radar antenna, moving right, left, center, and back, again. Periodically, look far out across the water to detect tailing fish, wakes, birds, or any other signs of activity.

Most fish are on the move, so you must try to pick out any movement. That's not easy when the boat is being poled. Species such as the barracuda will lie motionless. There are instances where bonefish, tarpon, and other species will not be underway for reasons known only to them. That's why concentration is so important. Don't count on seeing the whole fish every time. You may only see a portion of it or a shadow. The silver sides of a shallow water denizen may look black or they may appear to be transparent. Bottom type and light help to camouflage those critters.

If a fish is relatively high in the water or if the water is very shallow, you will see a wake. A number of factors determine how pronounced the wake will be. It could be as indiscernible as a ripple moving across or against the tide. Those wakes often save the day when visibility prevents one from seeing beneath the surface. Even on bright days, you can often pick out a wake at a considerable distance and know that fish are coming your way or have time to move the boat and head them off.

When a fish picks a morsel off the bottom, it creates a small puff of mud. Experienced eyes identify this very slight discoloration in the water and know that something was just there. They look for fresh puffs of mud and then cast right in the area. The results can be impressive.

THE MOMENT OF TRUTH

Nothing is more demanding than to make a cast to a moving target without much time to get ready and have the lure or bait land in the right place. Speed and accuracy of presentation hold the key. You have to get it there now and there is no margin for error. The cast is all yours; it's one-on-one with nobody else to blame for inaccuracy.

There are basic rules. Wait until you are comfortable and make the first cast count. You may not get a second shot. If the fish turns or the cast goes astray, reel in as quickly as you can and make another cast. Do not try to turn a poor presentation into a good one; it doesn't work. Like duck hunting, you must maintain a lead. If you have reasonable eye-hand coordination, you'll do fine. Experts often pick a spot ahead of the fish and focus their eyes on it, still watching their quarry out of peripheral vision. This helps to get the right lead.

The most successful anglers eyeball the fish and their lure at the same time, trying to bring the two together. Predators are not normally charged by their prey, so the offering must look as if it is trying to escape or it was just flushed by the cruising fish. This often leads to misunderstanding. The angler sees the lure as passing in front of the fish, but the fish views the lure as coming toward it which is unnatural behavior.

The ideal cast is in front of and beyond the target. Then, before the cruiser gets close, reel the bait or lure until it is directly in front of the fish rather than on the far side. When you start the retrieve, it will look to the fish as if the goodie is trying to get away and that's all it usually takes. If your quarry doesn't react instantly, it means the bait has not been seen or the fish doesn't want it. Reel in and make another cast. Each time you offer the lure, pick the spot in advance. A bonefish, for example, feeds into the tide. That animal expects its food to be moving with the flow of water.

All of these problems are compounded when there is a school of fish. Keep in mind that a school takes on the role of a single superfish. If one member is spooked and bolts for safety, they all go. Whenever possible, pick out all of the fish before you make the first cast. If the lure lands on an unseen fish, the line crosses the back of a critter between you and the target, or anything else happens, you're back to square one after the water settles down.

There will also be times when one or more fish are moving directly away from you and it's improbable that you can head them off with the boat. You'll have to make a long cast and you don't want the line to land across the fish's back. Pick an area to one side or the other and try to work the lure past the fish a foot or two away. Vision is always best at right angles to the eye and your quarry may veer off to strike.

WADING

Whether the goal is striped bass in the northeast or bonefish in the Florida Keys, there is a special thrill and an added dimension in wading. It's as basic and challenging as fishing can get.

In cooler waters, chest-high waders become the uniform of the day, but in the tropics, anglers often walk around in shorts. At no time should anyone wade barefooted. The spiny sea urchin, coral, and other sharp things await the soft skin of an unshod foot. Sneakers will work, but the neoprene boots of the diver are an impressive choice. They cling tightly to the leg, preventing sand and silt from filling the foot portion.

Regardless where you fish, move slowly. In murky water, test the footing before the next step. Trying to swim in waders is difficult at best. When the water is clear, you want to spot fish before you ease up on them, so take the time to look carefully before each step. Above all, don't splash and don't make noise.

If you fish the shallows long enough, you'll find times when the water is too skinny for the boat to navigate and there are fish in front of you tailing all over. Make it a rule to always carry wading shoes when you fish the flats. Then, it's easy to put them on, slip over the side, and chase the fish.

As a word of caution, some flats are hard, but others are soft. Make sure of the bottom before you step in and find yourself waist deep in muck trying to struggle free.

Fishing the flats is a very special phase of the sport. It is a total experience where the actual hookup and subsequent battle are almost anticlimatic. Newcomers should always seek a guide until they begin to understand the parameters of this form of angling. Learning to spot fish and then make an accurate presentation becomes a goal in itself.

Shallow water angling has an addictive nature. It is demanding, requires concentration, and, at times, can be frustrating. At the end of the day you'll be tired, but refreshed and you won't have another thought in your head.

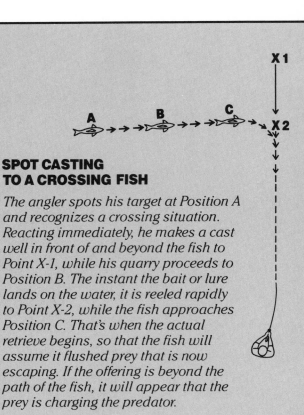

SPOT CASTING TO A CROSSING FISH

The angler spots his target at Position A and recognizes a crossing situation. Reacting immediately, he makes a cast well in front of and beyond the fish to Point X-1, while his quarry proceeds to Position B. The instant the bait or lure lands on the water, it is reeled rapidly to Point X-2, while the fish approaches Position C. That's when the actual retrieve begins, so that the fish will assume it flushed prey that is now escaping. If the offering is beyond the path of the fish, it will appear that the prey is charging the predator.

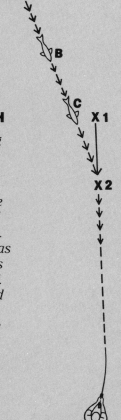

SPOT CASTING TO AN APPROACHING FISH

Seeing a fish approaching from Position A, the fisherman quickly makes his presentation to Point X-1, which is in front of the target and slightly beyond the projected line of travel. During the cast, the fish has closed to Position B and is moving toward Position C. The bait is hurriedly reeled to Point X-2 (directly in front of the fish) before the retrieve begins. Any movement of the offering toward one's quarry will usually flush it.

FLY FISHING: TECHNIQUE OF OPPORTUNITY

lt water fly fishing covers a broad spectrum of angling
allenges from mackerel, bluefish, striped bass, and tuna to
nefish, tarpon, and billfish. Put in proper perspective, it is
portunity sport that hinges on the species and conditions.
e snickers and laughter of yesteryear that once greeted the
ht wand aficionado on the marine scene have virtually
sappeared. The flyrod has finally arrived and has been
cognized as an effective tool.

If you can accept fly tackle as simply another way to fish
d have fun, getting into it is relatively easy no matter what
ters you travel. There are those who become so addicted
d obsessed that they worship a hunk of hackle or hair on the
d of a leader tippet as the only meaningful method. For the
st of us, the flyrod has its place. Keep one rigged and ready
enever you're out and you'll have many chances to use it,
tching an impressive share of fish in the process.

GETTING STARTED

In all other forms of casting, the weight of the lure or
rminal tackle pulls the line off the reel. It's just the opposite
fly fishing. The weight is in the flyline, and the fly, itself,
mains relatively weightless. You cast the line and the line
rries the fly to the target. Depending on the type of line you
lect, it also takes the fly to the proper depth.

Putting the right outfit together won't cause a problem if
u ignore the obvious and start from the other end. Most
glers insist on choosing the rod first and then adding a line
at matches the rod. The place to begin is with the size flies
eded to catch the most common species for which you
pect to fish. Once you know the approximate size of the
es, you can select a flyline heavy enough to carry those flies.
hen you have identified the line size, it's simply a matter of
cking a rod that matches that line.

To help you and to insure a semblance of uniformity
nong the various flyline makers, the American Fishing
ckle Manufacturers Association has established standards
r line sizes based on the weight of the first 30' in grains. They
ve assigned numbers ranging from 1 to 15 to represent the
rious size ranges. For most salt water use, you will be
ncerned with sizes 8 through 13.

Flylines are made in four basic shapes (designations are
own in parentheses): level (L), double taper (DT), weight
rward (WF), and shooting taper (ST). The basic salt water
e is a weight forward in which most of the weight is centered
the first 30' followed by a finer diameter running line.
ooting tapers are usually 30' long and are the same as a
eight forward except that the running line is not an integral
rt. It must be attached separately.

In certain marine situations and particularly on the clear,
allow flats of the tropics, it is often necessary to make a
ort, quick presentation. Experts reasoned that if the belly of
e weight forward line were shortened from 30' to 25', they
uld get a cast off with greater speed. That's how the "salt
ter taper" came into being and it is still on the market and on
e reels of anglers who don't recognize its shortcomings.
e salt water taper is a very difficult line to cast because it has
endency to "dump." Buy a standard weight-forward flyline

Wading with a flyrod for bonefish is one of the top angling challenges. Use small flies tied on #2 to #6 hooks.

and you have made the right choice. Shooting tapers are used
in situations where long casts are necessary to explore a lot of
water and in some situations with oversized, fast swimming
fish to reduce line drag. They offer their share of limitations as
well as advantages.

Flylines are manufactured in an assortment of densities,
enabling the user to reach various depths in the water column.
A floating flyline (F) remains on top of the water and is the
primary line when the water is shallow or fish are near the
surface. An intermediate line (I) sinks very, very slowly and
has become increasingly popular when there are weeds on
the surface or on windy days when wave action on a floating
line causes the fly to move erratically. There are several
densities of sinking lines (S) ranging from slow to high speed.
The high speed sinking lines contain plenty of lead in their
coating and they will reach a respectable depth. For maximum depth, specialists use 30' of lead core line and attach a
mono running line to it.

Depending on the manufacturer, a full flyline will be 82'
to 120' long. With few exceptions, a flyline over 80' or 90' is
superfluous. In fact, veterans often shorten the flyline to get
more backing on the reel or to help reduce line drag in the
water when a speedy fish is trying to escape.

You'll need backing behind the flyline to weather the run
of any critter. How much you use and the breaking strength
depends on the species. Dacron is the preferred material
because it lacks the stretch of monofilament and the choice is
usually 20-pound test for smaller fish or 30-pound for heavy-

weights. If you limit your fishing to mackerel, bluefish, redfish, trout, ladyfish, flounder, striped bass, and others that aren't known for long runs, 100 yards could be adequate. Bonefish, barracuda, permit, bonito, and so forth demand 200 yards of backing. If you are going to take on husky sharks, tarpon, billfish, and tuna, plan on at least 250 yards of 30-pound test Dacron backing.

Those who pursue trophy fish on heavy fly gear sometimes put 100 feet of 25-pound or 30-pound test monofilament between the flyline and the Dacron backing as a cushion. There is enough stretch in the mono to act as a shock absorber when the fish leaps, greyhounds, or simply surges. This is not a universal practice, but you should know about it.

Give or take a few inches, 9 feet ranks as the standard length for a salt water flyrod. There are some 10-footers on the market and they work well in specific situations such as wading for bonefish, but casting them can be a bit tiring. The flyrod must match the line. You'll find some designs where you can use a line one size heavier or lighter than the primary recommendation, but it is best to target the rod directly to the line. A 9-weight line should be cast on a rod rated as a number 9. Then, you might be able to go a size lighter or heavier if necessary.

Graphite has become the material of choice and there are now second generation graphites being offered. Material certainly helps performance, but design and engineering make a significant difference. All graphite rods are not great and some could not even be classed as good. You must ferret out the ones that cast best and have the necessary power to battle the fish once the hookup is achieved. There are also some excellent glass flyrods available at lower cost and particularly those made from S-glass which is lighter in weight and more responsive than the original E-glass.

On rods handling lines of 9-weight or heavier, a fighting butt helps to keep the reel away from the body when battling a fish. The fighting butt should have a rounded bottom for maximum comfort and not be more than about 2 inches in length. Longer butts only get in the way. If the butt is detachable, insert it in the rod before you go fishing. Trying to locate that butt and get it in place with a fish on the other end doesn't make much sense. A short butt does not get in the way when you are casting.

Some flyrod makers have been using ceramic guides and tiptops on their products. Research has shown that the largest snake guides available are probably the best choice. They offer the minimum resistance to the flyline and are large enough for knots to pass through. There is a tendency among some rod makers to use guides and tiptops with rings that are too small.

A flyreel must boast adequate line capacity for the flyline and the backing plus an exceptionally smooth drag. Traditionally, the single action flyreel in which one revolution of the handle produces one revolution of the spool is the primary choice. Automatic flyreels have little place in the marine environment and multiplying flyreels with gear ratios faster than one to one are not considered traditional by most enthusiasts.

An angler who isn't about to challenge tough, fast moving fish on fly certainly doesn't have to worry about more than a clicker for a drag that keeps the line from overrunning. Ext pressure can be applied with the fingertips on the spool rim on the bottom of the spool. Even a reel without a drag shou have a counterweight opposite the handle to keep the spo from chattering when the fish is taking line.

The choice of flyreels today is staggering and most them are excellent. Some models are extremely expensiv but they will also last a lifetime and perform well year aft year. Newcomers often wonder whether they should buy reel with right hand or left hand retrieve. If you are rig handed, reel with your right hand. The argument that you ha to change hands has little validity. Pumping a fish isn't t problem; you have to be able to recover line quickly and f long periods. That demands your primary hand on the re handle and not the rod. You can crank longer and faster wi your stronger hand. It is not the same as spinning where t weaker hand works the reel.

As you investigate the better reels, you'll find you have choice between direct drive (the handle turns backwa when line is stripped from the spool) and anti-reverse (whe the handle remains stationary). There are arguments for bo types. You certainly have an option with larger reels, but if y use a light drag on the smaller models, you may have troub recovering line with an anti-reverse reel.

UNIVERSAL TACKLE

Although the ultimate lies in matching tackle to t quarry and conditions, you can fish almost anywhere in t world for the majority of flyrod species using a 9-weight ou and one capable of handling a 12-weight or 13-weight. T 9-weight would be matched to a bonefish size reel that hol 200 yards of 20-pound Dacron backing plus a WF-9-F (weig forward, 9-weight, floating) flyline. The huskier outfit wou have a tarpon size reel that holds 250 yards of 30-pou backing plus a WF-13-F flyline. Capacity could be as much 300 yards.

For billfish, tuna, and other long running denizens, y can buy a billfish size reel that holds much more 30-pou backing plus the same flyline. The largest flyreels are bu and cumbersome, making them more suitable for very sp cific situations.

Fly fishermen quickly develop a concern for lightness their equipment, often announcing the weight of the rod ounces and fractions. Actually, weight is relative, particula when you attach a heavy reel to the butt. What you really ne is a rod that casts well and a reel with the strength, capaci and drag to do the job.

THE BUSINESS END

The purpose of the leader lies in keeping the flyline aw from the fish. In clear, shallow water where the fish are skitti you need a longer leader; with sinking flylines or on chop days, you can do well with a shorter leader. A butt section relatively heavy monofilament is attached to the flyline with nail knot or via interlocking loops in the end of the flyline a the butt section. The length of the butt section ranges fro half the length of the total leader to almost two-thirds.

The tippet (or class tippet) represents the lightest secti of the leader and is a length of mono up to 16 pound test. must break before the backing or you could lose a flyline in t rocess if the drag on the reel is not set correctly. When ~~fi~~shing for species that could abrade the leader or cut it with ~~th~~eir dentures, the practice is to add a shock tippet of 12 ~~in~~ches. This shock tippet is made from heavier mono when ~~ab~~rasion is the problem and with stainless steel wire for toothy ~~d~~enizens. The strength and abrasion resistance of the shock ~~d~~epends on the species. You don't need much for a fish that ~~m~~ay rub its nose on the bottom to get rid of the hook, but ~~ta~~rpon, billfish, and other critters require a serious shock ~~le~~ader of 80-pound or 100-pound test.

Thousands of fly patterns have been developed over the ~~y~~ears, but you only need a few basic styles to catch fish. Most ~~sa~~lt water species feed on small fish, so patterns represent ~~b~~ait. On the flats, crustacea are added to the diet, tempting ~~ti~~ers to imitate shrimp and crabs. There is also the choice of ~~to~~pwater poppers that make a surface commotion.

Experience and local advice will help you select the ~~st~~arting patterns and colors. Keep a few principles in mind. ~~Si~~ze is important. Some species feast on offerings an inch or ~~tw~~o long, while others want more of a mouthful. Pick a size ~~an~~d silhouette that tempts the species you hope to catch.

Hook size plays a vital role. For one thing, it is difficult to set a hook over 5/0 with a flyrod. Use smaller hooks for most flies and match the hook to the fly and the species for which it is intended. Then there is sink rate. A fly has to get down to fish-eye level and some patterns sink faster than others. In skinny water, just the reverse is true. You want a fly that hovers and lingers. Palmer-tied offerings with plenty of hackle wrapped around the hook shank hold a fly in suspension.

Castability becomes another critical factor that people sometimes ignore. You have to be able to cast the fly to the fish. If it is big and bulky, wind resistance reduces distance quickly. Certain patterns simply cast better than others. Until you get the fly where the fish can see it, you don't stand a chance.

LEARNING TO CAST

Casting a fly takes practice and the place to learn is on the lawn or in a nearby park. Waiting until you are on the water in a fishing situation will only cause frustration and aggravation. If your tackle is balanced (line weight matches the rod) and you have a well-engineered rod, mastering the cast should not be difficult. Try to find someone locally who has the skill to teach you and ask him to help. Learning to present a fly properly brings a sense of satisfaction that overshadows the rewards from other angling techniques. It is worth the effort.

In addition to other instructions you might receive, a few key pointers will help significantly. Start with the rod tip an inch or two above the surface of the water. This is essential, although it is constantly overlooked by good casters. The first part of rod movement takes the slack out of the flyline. You simply cannot make a cast before the fly starts to move. Lifting the rod tip vertically before you begin the backcast works wonders in removing the slack and insures a crisp backcast.

The same theory applies to the forward cast. Ignore those advocates who tell you that you have to stop the backcast at eleven o'clock, twelve o'clock, or any other time. Once you make the backcast, you want the rod extended well behind you and parallel to the water. That gives you a broad arc to remove any slack as the rod starts its forward motion.

Controlling the cast combines two factors. The direction in which you stop the rod will determine where the fly will go and the tighter the loop, the more control you will have. Loop control is a function of wrist movement at the completion of the cast. The shorter the distance in which the wrist is stopped, the tighter the loop. The cast is actually the same as you would make with a spinning or bait casting outfit, except with that tackle there is no loop. When you have to drive a cast into the wind or you want to put the fly on a specific target, a tight loop is essential.

FLY FISHING

Fly fishing takes two basic forms: one either casts and retrieves without seeing the quarry or holds the fly in hand and only makes a presentation when the fish is in sight. Casting to a moving target demands speed and accuracy just as it does with other tackle. If you are in a situation where you will be casting to fish that you see, strip out just enough flyline to cover the longest cast you anticipate making. As you get ready, make one practice cast. This puts the flyline in the correct position to shoot. Otherwise, the line from the bottom of the pile will try to come up first and a tangle will ensue.

~~Si~~ght casting with a flyrod means that you hold the fly in your ~~ha~~nd and wait until the target is identified. A forward, aerial ~~fa~~lcast gets the line moving prior to the backcast and presen~~ta~~tion to the fish. If you're new to the game, practice this ~~te~~chnique before you fish the flats.

Whether you are blind casting or spot casting, the flyline should be shooting through your line hand so you can stop it at any time by clamping your fingers on it. As the fly is about to land on the water, transfer the line under the first finger of your rod hand so that it is positioned under the foregrip of the rod.

Before you start to strip, the rod tip should be low to the water pointing directly at the fly and the rod butt at your belt buckle. Reach behind the forefinger of your rod hand and grasp the line with the fingers of your line hand. By pulling the line toward you, you cause the fly to move. The length of the pull determines how far the fly will move and the frequency of the pulls how fast it will move. A smooth pull makes the fly swim, while a quick jerk causes it to hop somewhat erratically.

By keeping the rod tip low to the water and pointing at the fly, you are in position to make another cast or set the hook if a fish should strike. Remember that the weight of the line is in the first 30'. Unless you can see a fish following the fly, it's time to make another cast when there is 30' of line on the water in front of you. This helps to eliminate false casts. A good caster can pick up 30' or 35' of line and shoot another 30' with a single backcast. That allows one to cover the water effectively with a minimum of effort.

SETTING THE HOOK

When a fish strikes, lift the rod sharply to set the hook or pull it low to the water on one side. With certain hard mouthed species such as tarpon, some guides insist it is better to simply hold the rod and line tight until the fish literally tears the line out of your hand. Whatever method you use, your first concern is the loose flyline at your feet. With a small fish that cannot take much line, this may not pose a problem and you

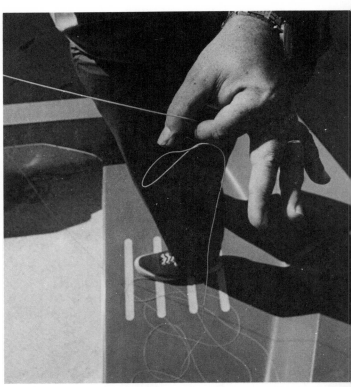

Once you set the hook with a flyrod, worry about the loo[se] line at your feet. Make an extra guide with the thumb a[nd] forefinger of your line hand and lead the line off the deck.

might be able to strip the fish in using the same syste[m] recommended for retrieving the fly.

Most marine denizens pack enough strength to take li[ne] Direct your attention to the loose line at your feet. With t[he] thumb and forefinger of your line hand form a circle arou[nd] the line and use it to lead the line through the first guide of t[he] rod. Once the fish is on the reel, you are ready to start t[he] battle. If the fish does not take all of the line, shift the rod [to] your line hand, clamp the line under the forefinger, and reel [in] the slack.

WHEN TO USE THE FLYROD

Dedicated aficionados set out to catch certain speci[es] on fly and prefer that tackle when the wind is somewhat und[er] gale force and they are wading or aboard a boat where t[he] others don't mind the use of fly gear. For the majority [of] people, the flyrod represents opportunity sport. Newcome[rs] do best when they rely on spinning, trolling, or bait casti[ng] gear to locate the fish and catch enough to be satisfied. The[n] they produce the fly outfit, knowing there are fish in the are[a.]

Fly fishing on the shallow flats of the tropics has becom[e] a way of life. In deeper water, it pays to look for breaking fi[sh] or go with someone who can tease the fish to the fly with li[ve] bait or a hookless chugger. Chum slicks are an ideal place [to] learn to use the fly. Make a short cast, strip some line, and l[et] the fly drift through the slick without any movement. Su[r]prisingly, fish will pick it up on the dead drift and you'll see t[he] line come tight.

Wherever you use a flyrod, it will bring an extra measu[re] of fun and each small success will begin to loom as a maj[or] angling victory.

A finger placed on the spool of a flyreel or on the rim will serve as a brake or drag. Additional pressure can be added with this method, even when the reel has a built-in drag.

ON FOOT

Millions of anglers on all coasts find fishing afoot to be fun and productive. They ply the high surf, scale the jagged jetties, lean over piers and bridges, stand on sea walls and along canal banks, and test the terrain around commercial docks. Wherever water brushes the landscape, someone will be trying to catch fish. Each individual chooses how relaxing or serious he wants to make this type of sport. The opportunities and potential for outstanding action are certainly there.

Like any other angling pursuit, tides, seasons, time of day, and a host of other factors determine where the fish will be and when. Regulars consistently score better than the casual visitor, suggesting that local knowledge and experience make a significant difference.

THE HIGH SURF

Nothing seems more soul-satisfying than the tangy smell of salt air, crashing seas, and the sizzle of white water as a wave recedes. From the rockbound shores of Maine to the gentle beaches of the Gulf and back around to the Pacific Coast, dozens of species invade the surf to scout for forage. The dedicated angler waits patiently for flurries of activity, relishing in the occasional blitz when full scale war erupts virtually at his feet.

Whether you fish on foot or log countless miles driving on the sand in a buggy, learning the water holds the key to consistent success. Any beachfront has its share of structure with holes, pockets, rocks, reefs, sloughs, cuts, and other configurations that hold baitfish and gamesters. Pick a period of extreme low tide during the new or full moon (spring low tide) and study the beaches you plan to fish regularly. Take a pencil and paper and draw diagrams. If you have a camera, make pictures of each area and file the prints in a notebook so that you can refer to them at any time. This type of preparation brings its own rewards.

As you study the surf, focus on anything different from its surroundings. A rock or two jutting out of the sand could be a dynamite spot on half an incoming tide. There may be a deeper hole where bait will gather on falling water. Above all, it is essential to locate sloughs running parallel to the beach. Frequently, there is a slough, a bar, slough, bar, and deep water or any combination of the above. These lateral highways become thoroughfares for forage species and the gamefish charge through the area in search of food. At the same time, note that these sloughs eventually tail off into a channel that moves seaward. This is critical territory and you should remember it well.

If you don't scout the beach on low water, there are other

Nothing pumps up enthusiasm faster than a bluefish blitz on a northern beach. The action seldom lasts long, but the rewards are worth the wait.

clues. The higher on the beach a wave breaks, the deeper the water in front of it. Places where waves run farther up the sand indicate deeper water. Study the wave patterns. A break in a rolling surf may indicate a deep channel going seaward. Learning to read water will help you to locate fish. Memory is tricky. Keep a notebook handy and take notes. It may prove invaluable on another day.

The best time to fish may be when you are on the water, but an incoming tide usually produces better results in the surf. In fact, from a half tide to high water and the first of the outgoing should be prime time. There are plenty of exceptions. All of us have seen husky predators slip into very shallow water on low tide, attacking baitfish a few feet from damp sand. Being observant is essential. Look for boils, swirls, or even a glimpse of a fish in the waves. If you see a school of bait, watch it closely; sooner or later its presence will be discovered. Bird activity is an obvious tipoff. Carry binoculars and use them regularly.

Where the sand shoulders an inlet, outgoing tide ranks as first choice. The current will sweep bait seaward and the fish you want to catch line up to feast on the smorgasbord. They may shift positions on various tidal stages, but they should be on hand. Just as fish count on the wave action of the surf to tumble and disorient bait, they also rely on bars at inlet mouths to funnel the bait toward them. Each species has its own

Catching a trophy channel bass or red drum out of the surf is always an exciting adventure. This one ate a whole finger mullet anchored to the bottom.

patterns which should be learned.

For many, surf fishing is a relaxing pastime. They walk o drive to a spot they consider productive, set out the san spikes, and pitch a temporary camp. Most are content to pu bait on the bottom and wait for a strike. Special sinker design hold better in the surf and the rig remains planted in th tumbling, churning water. More aggressive anglers rely o light sinkers and let the bait sweep along the bottom. To then casting again and again is fun and not a chore.

The truly serious surfcaster works artificials most of th time and he walks great distances casting and retrievin Everything he needs is carried in a pack hung from his waist o slung over his shoulder. A rain top and waders become th uniform of the day.

Not every situation demands the long surf sticks. Angle fishing sloughs along the Outer Banks for Spanish mackere weakfish, and similar species sometimes rely on light spinnin or bait casting. The barred surf perch in California is a perfe target for ultra light enthusiasts until a corvina comes alor and creates a surprise. At the other extreme, the mullet run i Florida and along the Gulf Coast forces anglers to spoo heavier line. Battling a tarpon over 100-pounds from the san challenges even the most skillful. There are a handful of su specialists who land sharks of several hundred pounds fro the beach regularly.

There is a belief among some surfman that every ca must probe seaward at maximum distance. That may be tru when it is essential to reach a particular slough or cut, but the are more fish taken regularly inside of a long cast. Bait uses th shallows of the surf for protection and that's where gamefis have to go if they want to find food. They'll chase their pre right up on the sand, if necessary. For that reason, diagon casts and those parallel to the beach often do a better job tha those aimed at the horizon. Work the beach sensibly ar systematically and you should do as well as anyone.

Landing a fish in the suds takes a bit of understanding ar practice. The first rule dictates that you stay opposite yo adversary. If the fish swims to the right or left parallel to th beach, run down the sand in the same direction, so the lir points directly seaward to the fish.

In the final stages, use the wave action to help you. Tryir to drag a fish against receding water proves foolish and cou break a line or pull a hook. Work your quarry on the back of wave and tow the fish shoreward with the help of the sea. that wave breaks, wait for the next. Finally, pick the wave, kee the line tight, and move away from the water's edge. Swim th fish with the wave. When the wave breaks and the water dro back, your fish will be flopping on moist sand.

JETTIES AND ROCKS

Man-made jetties formed from massive rocks jut seawa in an attempt to protect the sandy beaches from erosion b wave action or shoulder the straight channel of an inle Concrete walkways atop some jetties provide easy access, b other rockpiles show the ravages of countless storms ar crashing waves powerful enough to rearrange boulders int grotesque configurations.

Fishing from jetties and rocks represents specialize sport and specific equipment. Safety dictates that you alwa ish the more treacherous areas with a partner. One must constantly be aware of sea and tide conditions. It's easy to work your way out on low, incoming water and then suddenly discover that the flood tide and surging surf have cut off your escape route. When waves are breaking over the end of a jetty, that's no place for mortal man. Spray is one thing; seas are another.

The green and black coloration on rocks are caused by algae and other growths. Many of these plants have a coating of slime to keep them from drying out at low tide. A banana peel would rank in the non-skid category compared to the slickness of jetty rocks. Ignore the claims of boot manufacturers. No sole has a prayer of holding on these rocks regardless of design. The answer lies in ice creepers or a similar device slipped over a boot foot or made an integral part of it. The fewer points of metal that touch the rock, the better. Without proper footwear, stay off rocks and jetties. There is no compromise.

Jetty jocks opt for medium length surf rods ranging from 8' to 9', which are long enough to work around the rocks, but not cumbersome to carry and handle. Inexperienced anglers plod forward to the end of the jetty and want to win a distance tournament with their casts. Rocks provide a sanctuary for baitfish. The action usually occurs right around the structure rather than in open water.

Skilled regulars move to their favorite spots first and insist that the initial casts are the most important. They don't make these at random, preferring to toss bait or lure to the precise spots where they think the fish will be holding. If you haven't tried a particular jetty, start somewhere around the middle and fan your casts in both directions. Move out a bit and repeat the process. Don't overlook the pocket formed by the jetty with the beach.

Rocky coastlines produce challenges similar to those on a broken and battered jetty. The same caveats apply including the use of ice creepers for traction and footing. On both the Atlantic and Pacific Coasts, anglers now don wetsuits and scamper among the rocks like seaside versions of mountain goats. They reach spots inaccessible to most and catch fish in the process, but it is a game reserved for the athletic and the agile.

Landing a fish from rockpiles or jetties taxes the imagination at times. Veterans pick the sites in advance where they can get down to the water's edge without being dashed against the rocks in the process. They lead the fish after the battle to these exact locations before slipping down to gaff or release their quarry. During the fight, it is vital to stay opposite the fish. That may necessitate some hasty scrambling, but the outcome hangs in the balance. If the line brushes against a rock, the brawl will end abruptly in the fish's favor. That's why an 8' or 9' rod helps.

At night, a miner's type light worn around the neck and pointed downward is the preferred choice. Lights that shine in the water will scare fish, so you want to keep the beam aimed at your hands or your feet. Jetty aficionados often wear hip boots with a rain suit over them rather than chest waders. It's a matter of personal preference. As a safety precaution, an inflatable life jacket or a flotation jacket might come in handy in an emergency.

The high surf has always held a fascination for fishermen. Miles and miles of beachfront provide fishing opportunities for both the serious and casual angler.

PIERS

A pier provides a path above the waves to walk seaward and fish without getting one's feet wet or having to muscle up to breaking water. The structure gains support from an intricate, crisscrossed labyrinth of pilings and struts, which double as a haven for schools of bait. Less formidable piers stretch into bays and other bodies of water solely for fishing.

Easy access and a nominal charge make a commercial pier appealing to beginning fishermen, but it also attracts its share of regulars who invariably secure the choice spots. Most piers sell bait, tackle, and even support a snack bar for the hungry and thirsty. No fishing location proves consistently productive around the clock, but those fishing from piers do enjoy flurries of activity.

To protect patrons, casting areas may be restricted on a pier with most of this activity limited to the far end, which often forms a T. If you do cast away from the structure, be sure to check behind you before you swing your arms forward. It is also customary to announce that you are "going out" before you actually make the cast.

If the water around the pier is somewhat clear, the high vantage point gives you a chance to scout the area while wearing polarized sunglasses. As you gain experience, you should be able to spot fish in the water. There is a natural tendency to gravitate to the far end of the pier and deeper water. At times, this could be the only place where the action is taking place. However, it's worth checking the inshore sectors that seldom receive much attention. You can never tell what may be around.

Natural baits get most of the play, but a few veterans bounce leadheads or cast plugs from a pier. If you are going to bottom fish, use the freshest bait you can. Buy your bait on site if they have quality offerings; otherwise, pick it up at a tackle shop on your way. Live bait sometimes performs miracles when fished from a pier. Carry a light outfit and the right bait to catch smaller fish from the pier. Then, rig the live bait on a huskier rod and put it out there. Use a float or balloon to keep it at a regulated depth or simply live line it directly.

It pays to be ready for any eventuality. Take along a choice of baits, two or three outfits, and enough terminal tackle and artificials to counter any situation that might arise. A few judicious questions to the pier operator over the telephone should bring you the information you need.

Not all of the action takes place away from the pier. Gamefish frequently navigate among the pilings or along the edge looking for food. At night, predators lurk in the shadows on the edge of the light. Anglers with casting outfits use artificials to probe these areas. A handful of specialists arrive at uncrowded times and walk the railing looking for signs. When they spot activity, they'll drop a lure beyond the target and work it through the zone.

Piers make great training grounds for kids, while offering bathroom facilities, food, and drink. If you do take the youngsters, concentrate on the smaller species. They become more excited over continuous action than they do wrestling with some oversized trophy after an excessively long wait.

BRIDGES

Bridges cross inlets and estuaries throughout coastal areas. The more obvious ones receive plenty of attention, but there are countless spans traveled by cars daily that seem to be ignored by anglers. An obscure crossing over relatively shallow water may become a hotspot under certain tidal conditions.

A growing number of bridges have been ruled off limits to fishermen because of the danger of vehicular traffic. Each year, excited anglers step back to set the hook and wind up in front of a fast moving auto or truck. Catwalks have been constructed on some spans, but they always seem to be in the wrong place. There is a trend in some parts of the country to leave old bridges standing as fishing piers when a replacement bridge is opened.

Bottom fishing occupies the interests of many bridge regulars. Their efforts are directed toward the more common fare in the area, ignoring the prized gamefish that sometimes cruise around the pilings and supports. When a tidal flow is present, these fishermen favor the down current side so that their offerings are carried away from the structure. At slack tide, they enjoy the brief opportunity of fishing close to the bridge, although some shun this and continue to cast away from the natural cover.

Those searching for predators such as striped bass, tar-

pon, snook, and other species favor the upcurrent side of th[e] bridge. As the flowing water strikes the supports, a dead spot [is] created similar to the effect of a rock in a stream. Fish usual[ly] station themselves in these specific spots out of the flow an[d] wait for food to be swept toward them. With a few powerf[ul] tail strokes, they can ease out, engulf the prey, and then let th[e] current carry them back to their lie. If the right water cond[i]tions exist close to the bridge abutments, the wing walls mak[e] excellent casting platforms.

When fishing the uptide side, casts should be mad[e] diagonally across and allowed to sweep back toward th[e] bridge. It takes some pretty careful monitoring of the line [to] retrieve the bait or lure before it swings under the span. Whe[n] hooked, a few species will struggle against the current an[d] swim away from the bridge. Unfortunately, other critters pref[er] to go with the flow and they can be on the otherside before yo[u] gain control.

Regulars bent on landing these oversized fish resort to [a] technique known as bridge trolling. They use stout rods wit[h] the heaviest line they can handle. Reel drags are locked in th[e] exterminate position in preparation for the tug-of-war that wi[ll] certainly ensue. Live bait is a favorite, but a rigged, dead ba[it] works and swimming plugs have been known to take the[ir] share of fish. The offering is dropped to the surface of th[e] water and held there. With the rod extending over the rail lik[e] an outrigger, the angler walks up and down, dragging th[e] goodie on the surface.

When a strike comes, it is awesome and explosive. This [is] a do-or-die situation. Every effort is made to keep the fish[']s head above water while it struggles. If the technique [is] successful, the tired critter is dragged the length of the bridg[e] and landed from the wingwall. On longer bridges, a speci[al] gaff consisting of a treble hook and shower clip (to slip aroun[d] the line) will be lowered to the fish. Bridge trolling prove[s] particularly effective at night and accounts for some troph[y] specimens.

The lights from a bridge create a shadow line after dark. [If] gamefish are around, they will surely line up on the edge of th[e] shadow, peering into the lighted area. Bait may be attracted t[o] the lights and that's all it takes to start the activity. From [a] fishing standpoint, you want your offering to start in the brigh[t] area and sweep back toward the shadows. Get ready, becaus[e] a strike could come at any time.

Fishing on foot offers countless options and has i[ts] rewards. Casting a shoreline, walking a nearby bridge, work[ing] a seawall, or standing on a dock after the day's activity [is] over can be done easily without much preparation. It's th[e] type of sport that lends itself to an hour or two before or aft[er] work. That can also be said of surf fishing and rock scram[bling, although the latter two often demand a bit more prepa[a]ration and time depending on the area. If you live near th[e] beach, the world of the sea is yours.

Anglers ignore the fact that big fish frequently show i[n] areas overlooked by the majority. You don't always need [a] boat to reach the heart of the action. It's amazing what can b[e] done from shore if you take the time to learn the local wate[r] and do a bit of experimenting. Try those spots you've alway[s] passed up on various tidal stages. They suddenly may becom[e] a deep secret that you guard jealously.

FOR THE TABLE

Quality and freshness are two factors that seafood lovers come to expect from their dinners. Although we sometimes take a moist fillet for granted, there is often a painstaking amount of care involved in its preservation. Simply pitching a fish into an unprepared box and not worrying about it until it's ready for the cleaning table will drastically reduce its quality. Fishermen spend considerable amounts of money on boats and tackle as well as countless hours in pursuit of fish for sport or food. To simply allow a fish to spoil because of inadequate preparation is not only a waste of a natural resource, but inefficient planning on the captain's part. If a fish is removed from the water, a few simple procedures will insure its freshness.

ADVANCE PREPARATION

Just as a successful day on the water hinges on advance preparation of tackle, baits, and strategies, caring for your catch will also follow similar guidelines. There's nothing quite as critical to preserving a freshly caught fish than the temperature of the fish box, particularly during the summer. Depending upon the season and species of fish, you'll be taking an animal out of a comfortable water temperature, exposing it to air temperatures, and dropping it into a fish box where it will likely remain for several hours before being cleaned. Add the stress factor of being hooked and gaffed and a fish will begin to spoil immediately if a ship's hold is not frigid enough to keep it in check.

If at all possible, pack a fish box full of ice well before a trip. Trailer boaters are fortunate in that they usually have their rigs hooked up to their vehicles the evening before. Loading up with ice can be as simple as a short drive to a neighborhood convenience store. Boats berthed at marinas can be easily loaded up as well, although it will take a few hands to haul the ice to it from the vehicle. By packing the holds the evening before, cool temperatures will be more evenly distributed than by tossing in a few bags of ice that morning.

Shaved ice is best, when available. However, unless you're near an ice house or commercial fish processing plant, is virtually unattainable. Block ice is a strong second choice. Although never widely abundant, particularly the large blocks, a number of marinas and convenience stores carry the product at prices that are comparable to cubes. Because of its density, block ice retains its shape and lasts longer than most other forms. Always try to obtain the substantial blocks of about 25 pounds for the holds of large and most mid-size boats. They'll retain their temperatures much better than the smaller ones, and drop into the boxes virtually unaltered. Boats with smaller holds or portable coolers should opt for blocks weighing five or 10 pounds. Cubed ice should be used only as a last resort. They're smaller in density and will melt quickly if the hold isn't well packed with them, especially if a large fish is placed on top. Furthermore, few fishermen will go to the expense of solidly filling their holds with ice cubes. It often requires many bags of ice cubes to adequately fill an average size box, where it sometimes takes only three or four blocks to do a similar job. Those who go the cube route, unless they're in a small skiff or working out of a cooler, rarely go the distance in properly supplying a hold.

You can never head to sea with enough ice. Most commercial fishing fleets adhere to a standard requiring approximately five pounds of ice for every one pound of fish. Compared to large commercial boats that have the capacity to layer fish and ice, recreational anglers on small boats must stock their fish boxes full of ice and then worry about making room for a fish when it comes aboard. With block ice, layer the bottom of a hold, splitting additional units with a pick and packing them along the sides. If a separate box is available, pack that too. If need be, you can always dump ice at sea to make room for fish.

ICING PROCEDURES

When a catch becomes official, immediately place it in the box. If the holds are full of ice, lay the fish on the deck just long enough to make room for it. Always try to layer a fish between ice, making certain to avoid the bottom of the box. Any sludge from melted ice, slime, or blood will strongly flavor a fish that has been submerged in it. Commercial fishermen often add a limited amount of pure sea water, creating a near freezing brine that can keep fish fresh and in prime condition for several days. Brining is often used commercially and on long distance trips where there is a likelihood of remaining at sea for a substantial period of time. However, it also can be used by recreational anglers to keep their catch in optimum condition.

A captain who takes aboard little or no ice almost always runs the risk of spoiling his catch. As easy as it is to prevent, the number of anglers who leave the dock or boat ramp inadequately prepared is staggering. An afternoon spent at the local fish cleaning tables will indicate how predominant this problem really is. Well maintained fish will be moist and retain most of their natural coloration, while neglected fish will have a dry, colorless appearance. Furthermore, there are always one or two fishermen who catch a whopper, have no room in their fish box, and leave it on the deck. It usually comes to the fish cleaning table in a barely salvageable condition with sunparched, wrinkled skin and sunken eyes. The result of this

If you are going to keep your catch, protect the meat by packing the fish on ice immediately.

negligence will be a rather mushy flesh and a stronger than normal odor.

Although they shouldn't be relied upon on a regular basis, there are ways to help maintain a catch when there's an inadequate supply of ice. The primary goal is to keep the fish cool, reducing the rate of spoilage. Moisture within the cells of a fish help retain its freshness. When a fish is exposed to dry conditions, the flesh is drained of this critical moisture, and decomposition rapidly sets in. The best alternative to ice for retaining moisture is to place the catch in a box filled with salt water.

Whenever possible, it's best to circulate water through a well to keep temperatures constant. Without a circulation pump, it may require some work to rid any excess blood from the water which may effect the taste of the fish. Boxes that ride at sea level should have their drain opened to move the water while drifting or trolling. However, it may take a few running and stopping maneuvers to completely drain and refill the compartment. Coolers will require constant water changes.

With small fish such as trout and redfish, you may consider replacing any drinks or food in a cooler with them, providing there's ice. If there's a limited supply, try soaking a towel in salt water and wrapping it and any ice around the fish. The towel will help retain moisture, and keep the coolness directly on the fish. With a fish that's too large for a box, wash the deck to remove any dirt and to cool it down. If ice is available, either chip or crush enough of it to form a bed. It's sometimes difficult to evenly disperse block ice for this purpose, but give it a try. Once an icy layer is on deck, lay the fish on top and cover it with more ice, paying particular attention to the back and stomach segments. Moisten a towel with salt water and lay it over the fish. This will prevent direct exposure to the sun as well as retaining the moisture and holding the ice in place. Check and add ice as needed, making certain to keep the towel soaked with salt water.

With a large fish and no ice, it becomes extremely important to shelter it from sunlight. If there's a Bimini top or spray hood on the vessel, open it up and lay the fish in the shade. In extreme cases, it may pay to remove the top completely, laying it over the catch. However, make sure there's adequate ventilation to maintain cool temperatures. Use plenty of wet towels and constantly dump buckets of sea water on top of the fish every five minutes or so. The most logical solution would be to cut the trip short and run the trophy back to the dock, especially if it's to utilized for food.

CLEANSING THE HOLDS

Cleaning a fish box is important and vital to the quality of the fish and the health of the consumer. All fish contain bacteria in the form of a fine coating of slime. This bacteria protects the fish against infection from foreign substances and is completely harmless to humans, providing the catch has been properly handled. However, when such residue or blood is left unchecked in a fish box that has adequate moisture for growth, infectious (harmful) bacteria is likely to set in. If a fish box is not cleansed properly and thoroughly, bacteria will immediately infect the flesh of a freshly caught fish. In serious cases, illness may arise from consuming a contaminated fish.

After a hold has been unloaded and completely drained, rinse and thoroughly scrub it with a cleansing solution. Don merely throw in some soap and hose it out. Bacteria is no visible to the human eye, and it has a way of clinging stub bornly to a surface. Repeat the procedure a second time, an don't be afraid to add a shot or two of disinfectant before th final rinse. Store or cover the boat with the fish box lid removed or in the open position to draw out any moistur Closed lids are conducive to humidity and mildew. Trea portable coolers with the same respect.

GAFFING FISH

Gaffing a fish is an art that, when mastered, will ultimatel maximize the quality of fish that are kept for food. Naturall there will be situations where you'll have to take any shot at fish you can get to land it. However, always try to focus on fish's upper shoulders, just behind the gill plates. There are tw main reasons for this target's popularity. To begin with, you be able to effectively control the fish, retaining the ability t turn the gaff and alter its direction, a feat that's nearly impos ible with a tail shot. You'll also minimize the bleeding an damage only a limited amount of edible flesh.

Placing a gaff in the side or tail section of a fish w automatically destroy that area of meat. Since the flesh of fish is soft and will likely tear against the pull of the gaff, you run the risk of possibly damaging additional portions, as we as rupturing vital organs that are apt to saturate it with bloo And remember, it's the motion, not the force, that drives a ga home. When a fish comes into range, use a steady sweepir motion, lifting the fish up and into the boat. Never swing a ga like a baseball bat, looking for a home run hit.

Whenever possible, use a one handed lip or release ga that's intended for placement in a fish's lower jaw. Despite i compact size, it's very easy to use. A fish is simply led boatsid where the mate will take hold of the leader with one hand an with his other, insert the gaff, point first, in the fish's mouth ar out through the thin membrane of the lower jaw. The fish ca then be controlled enough to remove the hook and release or placed in the fish box abrasion free. However, a lip gaff not practical for all species. It should never be used on billfis and only by experienced anglers on fish with acute dentitio A sudden surge by a wahoo, bluefish, or barracuda can infli serious injuries on an unsuspecting angler.

BLEEDING FISH

Bleeding a fish right after it's caught is an ideal way insuring that its flesh will be of the highest quality, reducing even eliminating strong flavor. While any fish can be bled, th process is usually reserved for the oily and bloody texture species that would otherwise make for a mediocre meal best. This category includes the tunas, bonito, jacks, bluefis and kingfish.

After a fish is boated and has had ample time to sett down, lay it firmly on a cutting board and work a sturdy, sha knife from just above the pectoral fin down deep through th fish's throat. Repeat the procedure on the other side. You m even want to remove the head entirely and gut the fish at th point, making an incision from the anal opening to the thro This operation is best done overboard, but most fish seem be butchered in the cockpit. After the blood and entrails a removed, making sure that any blood pockets have be scraped out, wash the fish thoroughly with salt water. It is now ready to be iced. Pack the body cavity solidly with ice, and layer the fish with it. Follow this procedure and your catch will be in prime condition and a pleasure to consume afterwards.

STEAKING YOUR CATCH

Steaking involves a series of vertical cuts on a headed and gutted fish, producing semi-round cuts of meat that include a center bone. The style offers a quicker and easier alternative to filleting on long and slender species that don't require scaling such as kingfish, wahoo or swordfish.

After a fish has been gutted and headed, place it belly down on a cutting board. Secure the mid or tail section of the fish with one hand and begin steaking from the head back. On the first cut, work the knife to the backbone, feeling for a joint that will simplify separation. If you miss it, extra force will be required to slice through the backbone. From there on, leave about two inches between steaks until you approach the tail section. At this point, the steaks diminish in size and it's often best to fillet and skin the remaining portion. The best steaking knives will vary with the fish. However, you'll need a sharp one that's durable enough to cut through a backbone without any play. A knife of about six or eight inches is adequate for small to medium size fish, with a butchering knife reserved for the large species.

FILLETING YOUR CATCH

Filleting involves the separation of meat from a fish's backbone and skin (if desired). The best fillet knife is one that is very sharp and thin, with some flexibility built into it. Since you'll be slicing the meat away from a fish's backbone, you'll want the knife to contour along that column. Exactly how you approach the job of filleting a fish will vary somewhat with its size.

A small fish such as weakfish or mangrove snapper should be laid on its side. Making certain not to sever the backbone, work the knife in a somewhat crescent fashion beginning just behind the head, around the pectoral fin and down to the throat. Now, angle the blade so that it's almost flat with the fish, hugging the backbone as you slice down to the tail. Do not separate the meat from the tail. Firmly holding the fillet with your fingers or palm as you execute each side will make for a neater job. However, always grip the fish behind the knife blade to prevent injury. In addition, fillet a fish from the head to the tail. By doing so, you'll be working with the grain and not subject your hands to any painful puncture wounds from spines or fins.

At this stage, you'll have the opportunity to skin the catch. To do so, just flip the fillet over and, where it's connected to the carcass, lay the knife at an angle. Grab a section of skin just behind the knife and pull the meat past the stationary blade. You'll now have a skinless fillet. With experience, you'll also be able to work the knife forward while the meat is being pulled through, expediting the job. The fillet can also be separated from the carcass and skinned in similar fashion. Any trimming, such as removing the rib cage or blood line, should be done at this point. Complete the other side, and they're ready to be rinsed and stored.

Large fish such as dolphin, tuna, or grouper require a slightly different approach. Should you choose to skin the

To fillet a small fish, make a cut behind the head and pectoral fin. Select a sharp, flexible knife and work it carefully along the backbone.

To prepare a fish for baking or to cook a whole fish, remove the entrails and then cut off the head forward of the pectoral fins and behind the gill plates.

catch, it's often easier to accomplish this first. Position the fish on its side and outline it with a slight incision that's just deep enough to break the skin. Begin behind the head and round the pectoral fin, continuing to the tail just slightly above the belly and then up along the back. At the fish's shoulder, peel up enough skin to obtain a solid grip. Firmly hold the fish's head down with one hand, or have a friend help if it's an exceptionally large catch, and pull the skin from the meat. The skin usually separates with little difficulty. On smaller fish, the skin tag can actually be wrapped around a fillet knife's blade and peeled away by turning its handle. The knife also lends extra leverage.

After both sides have been skinned, run the forward edge of a knife down the backbone with a slight cutting motion. Work a similar pattern on the underside, beginning either above the rib cage to eliminate it, or down below it (if it's not prominent), and down to the tail. Slice the end of the meat from the tail, pulling the fillet back toward the head as you trim it from the backbone. If the rib cage is included, it can be trimmed out once the fillet has been separated. Complete the other side and section the fillets to your liking.

SCALING FISH

There are many species of fish, particularly panfish, that don't require skinning. In fact, the skin actually lends additional flavor to the fish and can help to form a heavy crust on those fried fillets. Furthermore, an outer layer of skin can prove beneficial when freezing fish for a lengthy period of time by helping to retain moisture and shield against freezer burn.

Fish with small, soft scales can be whisked clean in seconds with a sharp fillet knife. However, for safety reasons, the knife should be placed aside when it comes to dealing with those species carrying coarse, armor-like scales such as snappers or redfish. Trying to detach the scales with a thin bladed knife can result in slippage and possibly injure the cleaner. Fish scalers provide the optimum way of quickly and safely accomplishing the job. They are available in most tackle shops and appear similar to a hair brush that had its bristles replaced with a series of ragged, metallic edges.

WHOLE FISH

There will be certain fish that are too small to fillet or steak as well as some large ones which the angler may choose to bake whole. Dressing out a fish is very simple and probably the first method of cleaning a young angler learns when he breaks into the sport. Simply lay the fish on its side and remove the scales. With a sharp fillet knife or a stiffer version on large fish, remove the head from just behind the gill plates and discard. Make an incision from the anal opening forward, making certain to clean all viscera and blood sacs that may line the body cavity. Rinse thoroughly with fresh water. Make an incision along both sides of the dorsal fin, separating and removing it. The fish is now ready for preparation. As in all forms of fish cleaning, extreme caution should be taken to protect the hands and fingers from both the knife and a fish's spines, which can carry infectious bacteria. Fishermen may even want to invest in a fillet glove. Such hardware consists of cut-resistant materials that'll protect an angler from most cleaning accidents.

STORING YOUR CATCH

It's always best to eat fish as soon as possible to get the best taste. However, there are a few guidelines to follow to maximize freshness, if a fish is destined for the freezer.

An angler should decide approximately how much meat is ample for one table sitting as he cleans the catch. He should consider the size of his family and whether he'll occasionally want to fry up a slice or two for lunch. By packing his catch accordingly, and not merely lumping it together in one or two freezer bags, he'll reduce the amount of waste associated with leftover fish.

Fish that will be prepared a day or so after the catch can be kept fresh in the refrigerator, wrapped in aluminum foil. Fish likely to be consumed within a month or two can be wrapped in aluminum foil to seal in moisture, placed in an air tight bag and stored in the freezer. However, fish that will sit in a freezer more than two months should be prepared differently. Air is a main cause of freezer burn, and you must guard your catch from its perils.

Utilizing an air tight container, lay in a designated amount of fish and fill it with water. Place the top on the container and shake vigorously to remove excess air, cracking the lid t release it. By keeping fish submerged in water, a protectiv barrier of ice will form around it, practically eliminatin freezer burn. While tap water is sufficient, there are som variations that require brining as an added safeguard. A typic; brine solution will call for approximately a 1/3 cup of table sa to one gallon of water. For fish with a high fat or oil conter such as bluefish, kingfish or mackerel, it's been suggested th about eight tablespoons of ascorbic acid be substituted for th salt. The ascorbic acid, when mixed with a gallon of chille water, should prevent discoloration. Milk cartons or eve coffee cans (as a last resort) can be used to pack fisl However, the latter can lend a "tinny" flavor to fish.

TOOLS OF THE TRADE

There is no substitute for quality equipment when comes to cleaning your catch. An inferior knife will sure jeopardize the catch. Like most other fishing and boatii accessories, there are knives priced to fit within a wide ran of budgets. However, always opt for the best product you c. afford. The better knives offer a maximum of corrosion res tance and retain an edge longer.

Fillet knives are sharp, thin, and flexible and come various lengths. Their sole purpose is to precisely follow t contour of a fish's skeletal structure. The most widely us sizes in salt water are between six and 10 inches in length. Th can be used for a variety of cleaning situations and th narrow tip is particularly effective in scraping body caviti free of viscera. In contrast, a butchering knife is a large, hea bladed instrument designed for dressing out exceptiona large fish. Because of their length and rigidity, they make ide steaking knives. However, a fillet knife is commonly used conjunction with one. After a fish has been headed, a fil knife is often called upon to separate the meat from t backbone, trim the slabs into smaller portions, or to clean any steaks.

Practically all fishing knives have roots tracing back meat processing houses and restaurants. High-carbon blac work exceptionally well when sharp, but have problems w corrosion when subjected to a marine environment. Stainle steel knives are the best choice, since they hold up well in s water, can be honed incredibly sharp, and are quickly resh pened. Many models even offer a sheath which can attach an anglers belt, keeping the blade at the ready throughout t day.

Maintaining a sharp edge on a blade is critical in maxim ing a knife's effectiveness. Even the finest quality knives tend become dull after repeated use and an angler must rely o1 sharpening stone to file it back into shape. There are a numb of stones available ranging from commercial models to tho of only a few inches in length that fit conveniently withir tackle box.

A stone is usually lubricated with water or a honing oil reduce friction and facilitate sharpening. While a whetston great for retaining the edge of a knife that's in good conditic it may take an extra coarse abrasive stone to work ba damaged blades back into shape. Always rinse the knife af sharpening to remove oil and any metallic dust. A sharpeni stone also should be washed and dried before it's put away